ncw

KT-408-386

Human Rights

KEY CONCEPTS

Steve Bruce, *Fundamentalism*
Anthony Elliott, *Concepts of the Self*
Michael Freeman, *Human Rights*
John Scott, *Power*
Anthony D. Smith, *Nationalism: Theory, Ideology, History*

HUMAN RIGHTS

An interdisciplinary approach

Michael Freeman

polity

First published in 2002 by Polity Press in association with Blackwell Publishing Ltd.

Reprinted 2003 (twice)

Editorial office:
Polity Press
65 Bridge Street
Cambridge CB2 1UR, UK

Marketing and production:
Blackwell Publishing Ltd
108 Cowley Road
Oxford OX4 1JF, UK

Published in the USA by
Blackwell Publishing Inc.
350 Main Street
Malden, MA 02148, USA

ISBN 0-7456-2355-7
ISBN 0-7456-2356-5 (pbk)

A catalogue record for this book is available from the British Library and has been applied for from the Library of Congress.

Typeset in 10½ on 12 pt Sabon
by SNP Best-set Typesetter Ltd., Hong Kong
Printed in Great Britain by TJ International, Padstow, Cornwall

This book is printed on acid-free paper.
For further information on Polity, please visit our website:
http:// www.polity.co.uk

Contents

Acknowledgements   viii

1 **Introduction: Thinking about Human Rights**   1
   Realities   1
   Concepts   4
   The social sciences   6
   Beyond human rights law   8
   Conclusion   12

2 **Origins: the Rise and Fall of Natural Rights**   14
   Why history?   14
   On rights and tyrants   15
   Justice and rights   16
   Natural rights   18
   The age of revolutions   22
   The decline of natural rights   26

3 **After 1945: the New Age of Rights**   32
   The UN and the human-rights revival   32
   The Universal Declaration of Human Rights   34
   From theory to practice   42
      The cold war   42
      After the cold war   48
   Conclusion   51

4	**Theories of Human Rights**	55
	Why theory?	55
	Human rights theory	60
	Rights	60
	Other values	62
	Human nature	65
	Conflicts of rights	68
	Democracy	71
	Conclusion	73
5	**The Role of the Social Sciences**	76
	Introduction: human rights and social science	76
	The dominance of law	77
	Political science	78
	Sociology	83
	Psychology	90
	Anthropology	92
	International relations	94
	Conclusion	99
6	**Universality, Diversity and Difference: Culture and Human Rights**	101
	The problem of cultural imperialism	101
	Cultural relativism	108
	Minority rights	114
	Indigenous peoples	121
	The right to self-determination	123
	The rights of women	127
7	**Idealism, Realism and Repression: the Politics of Human Rights**	131
	The real politics of human rights	131
	The boomerang theory	134
	The national politics of human rights	138
	The statistics of human rights	140
	NGOs in world politics	142
8	**Development and Globalization: Economics and Human Rights**	148
	Development *versus* human rights?	148
	The right to development	151

Globalization   153
International financial institutions   160
Economic and social rights   164

9 **Conclusion: Human Rights in the Twenty-First
  Century**   **167**
Learning from history   167
Objections to human rights   172
Problems of intervention   174
Concluding remarks   176

References   179

Index   195

Acknowledgements

One evening in the autumn of 1977, Nick Bunnin, then teaching in the Department of Philosophy at the University of Essex, invited me to accompany him to a meeting of Amnesty International in Colchester. I agreed, reluctantly (for no reason other than laziness), but ended that evening as chairperson of the newly formed Colchester Group of Amnesty International. This book would never have been written were it not for Nick Bunnin and my colleagues – local, national and international – at Amnesty. I would like to remember particularly the late Peter Duffy, whose moral commitment and intellectual rigour made him an exemplary human-rights activist.

I hesitate to list those to whom this book owes an intellectual debt, for fear of omitting many unfairly. I would, nevertheless, like to thank Onora O'Neill, Sheldon Leader, Nigel Rodley, Françoise Hampson, Geoff Gilbert, Brian Barry, Alan Ryan, Albert Weale, Tom Sorell, the late Deborah Fitzmaurice, Matthew Clayton, Marcus Roberts, Andrew Fagan, David Beetham, Peter Jones, Simon Caney, Hillel Steiner, Bhikhu Parekh, Brenda Almond, Paul Gilbert, Peter Baehr, David Forsythe, Jack Donnelly, Rhoda Howard-Hassmann, Joseph Chan, Julia Tao, Will Kymlicka, Barry Clarke, Hugh Ward, John Gray and David Robertson.

I have learned a great deal from students in the Department of Government and the Human Rights Centre at the

University of Essex, far too numerous to mention. I have been invited to teach and learn about human rights in many countries, from China to Brazil, and cannot emphasize too much how important the ensuing cross-cultural dialogue has been.

None of the above is, of course, responsible for the errors in this book, which I have managed on my own. The book is dedicated to June, Saul and Esther with love and admiration. Without them, especially, it would not have been possible.

1
Introduction: Thinking about Human Rights

Realities

In March 1999 Lal Jamilla Mandokhel, a sixteen-year-old Pakistani girl, was repeatedly raped. Her uncle filed a complaint with the police. Police officers detained her attacker, but handed Lal Jamilla over to her tribe. The council of elders decided that Lal Jamilla had brought shame on the tribe, and that the only way to overcome the shame was to put her to death. She was shot dead on the orders of the council.

There are several shocking features of this story. They include the violent and humiliating crime committed against Lal Jamilla; the violence and unfairness of her punishment; and the complicity of the police in this injustice. This was not, however, an isolated incident. Hundreds of women and children are the victims of 'honour killings' every year in Pakistan. Their killers are rarely prosecuted, but even when they are convicted they often receive light sentences (Amnesty International 1999).

Lal Jamilla was the victim of an unjust custom, although agents of the state were accomplices to her killing. Many people in many countries have been direct victims of state violence in recent times. Government forces massacred more than half a million civilians in Indonesia in the mid-1960s in an attempt to suppress communism. Estimates of the number of people killed by the Khmer Rouge regime of Pol Pot in Cambodia vary between 300,000 and 2,000,000 (Glover 1999: 309). More than 9000 people 'disappeared' under the military government in Argentina in the late 1970s. During the rule of Idi Amin in Uganda from 1972 to 1978 more than 250,000 people were killed. Hundreds of thousands of civilians were murdered by security forces in Iraq during the 1980s. Almost 2 per cent of the population of El Salvador is estimated to have died as the result of 'disappearances' and political killings during the civil war between 1980 and 1992 (Amnesty International 1993: 2). In 1994 between 500,000 and 1,000,000 people were killed in the government-directed genocide in Rwanda (Glover 1999: 120). This list is far from complete. It does not include Bosnia, Chechnya, Kosovo, East Timor, and many other places.

The concept of human rights provides a way of thinking about such events. As you read these words, there will probably be reports in the newspapers, and on radio and television, of similar cruelties and injustices elsewhere. These are stories about the violation of human rights. These events are all too real, but 'human rights' is a *concept*. It is a device for thinking about the real, and expressing our thoughts. If we are to understand the discourse of human rights, we must analyse this concept, even though it is easier to respond with sympathetic emotion to stories like that of Lal Jamilla than to analyse our concepts so that they are clear and precise. The understanding of concepts is the goal of the philosophical discipline of *conceptual analysis*. The concept of human rights, however, presents a challenge to this discipline. Concepts are abstract, and conceptual analysis is an abstract discipline. It can seem remote from the experiences of human beings. The analysis of the concept of human rights, therefore, must be combined with a sympathetic understanding of the human experiences to which the concept refers.

If conceptual analysis is both necessary and problematic for understanding human rights, so is statistical analysis. R. J. Rummel has calculated that governments murdered at least 169,202,000 persons in the twentieth century. According to his estimates, more than 45,000,000 political murders occurred between 1945 and the early 1990s (Rummel 1994: chapters 1–2). These statistics are important, but they can easily numb our sense of the human suffering involved. Human-rights violations are facts that can be, and sometimes are, best expressed in terms of numbers, but there is an uneasy relationship between our knowledge of the numbers and our understanding of what they mean.

We do not need the concept of human rights to know and to say that these things are wrong. We do, however, need a *reason* to oppose them. If reality violates human rights, why should we take the side of human rights, and not that of reality? How do we know that there are any human rights? Such questions were posed, to challenge us, by the philosopher Jean Améry, who survived the Nazi extermination camp at Auschwitz. Perhaps, he considered, the Nazis were right because they were the stronger. Perhaps people had no rights. Perhaps all moral concepts were mere fashions. Was this not the reality of history? After all, classical Greek civilization was based on slavery and massacre. Was Nazi Germany different? (Glover 1999: 40).

Jonathan Glover has suggested that, for most people, most of the time, the virtues that matter are personal and narrow in scope. In everyday life, ordinary kindness is more important than human rights (Glover 1999: 41). Ordinary people, however, are sometimes not permitted an everyday life. They may get terror, massacres, mass rapes and 'ethnic cleansing'. The concept of human rights becomes relevant to ordinary people when the relative security of everyday life is absent or snatched away. It has often been said that human rights are most needed when they are most violated. Where they are generally well respected, we tend to take them for granted, and may consequently underestimate their importance.

The concept of human rights is, to a considerable extent, though not wholly, *legal*. The fountain-head of human-rights law is the Universal Declaration of Human Rights, which was adopted by the United Nations General Assembly on 10 December 1948. This declaration has, according to its historian, Johannes Morsink, 'profoundly changed the international landscape, scattering it with human rights protocols, conventions, treaties, and derivative declarations of all kinds.' There is now 'not a single nation, culture or people that is not in one way or another enmeshed in human rights regimes' (Morsink 1999a: x). The declaration was adopted in the aftermath of the victorious war against Fascism, and in a spirit of idealism. It makes a grand set of promises to the world's people. The declaration is said to be 'a common standard of achievement for all peoples and all nations'. All human beings, Article 1 affirms, 'are born free and equal in dignity and rights'. Everyone, Article 2 states, 'is entitled to all the rights and freedoms set forth in this Declaration without discrimination of any kind, such as race, colour, sex, language, religion, political or other opinion, national or social origin, property, birth or other status.'

There is obviously a wide gap between the promises of the 1948 declaration and the real world of human-rights violations. Insofar as we sympathize with the victims, we may criticize the UN and its member governments for failing to keep their promises. But we cannot understand the gap between human-rights ideals and the real world of human-rights violations by sympathy or by legal analysis. This requires investigation by the various social sciences of the causes of social conflict and political oppression, and of the interaction between national and international politics. The UN introduced the concept of human rights into international law and politics. The field of international politics is, however, dominated by states and other powerful actors who have priorities other than human rights. It is a leading feature of the human-rights field that the governments of the world proclaim human rights but have a patchy record of implementing them. We must understand why this is so.

Concepts

The concept of human rights raises further difficulties because it stretches well beyond cases of extreme cruelty and injustice. Article 1 of the Universal Declaration, for example, states that all human beings are equal in rights. Article 18 says that everyone has the right to freedom of religion. How should we define the right to freedom of religion of those whose religion denies that all human beings are equal in rights? How can we make sense of human rights if the implementation of some human rights requires the violation of others? Here the problem of implementing human-rights ideals derives, not from lack of political will or conflicts of political interests, but from the fact that human rights are not 'compossible', that is, the implementation of one human right can require the violation of another, or the protection of a human right of one person may require the violation of the *same* human right of another. If a religious group, for example, forbids its members, on the basis of its religious beliefs, to change their religion, then the religious freedom of the group will conflict with that of any members who wish to change their religion. If we support human rights that are not compossible, our thinking must surely be confused.

The problem of compossibility has been aggravated by what has been called 'rights inflation', that is, the extension of the concept of human rights to an ill-defined number of causes. There are controversial human rights even in the Universal Declaration, such as the right to 'periodic holidays with pay'. If the concept of human rights is to be useful, we must distinguish human rights from other social demands. Courts may decide rather precisely the legal rights of those who appear before them. Human rights are rather vaguely worded, and their meaning is not always settled in courts of law. Clarity in the understanding of human rights requires conceptual analysis, moral judgement and social-scientific knowledge. If the concept of human rights is to be useful, we must distinguish *human* rights from the *legal* rights of particular societies, and from other desirable social objectives.

What are 'rights', and how do 'human rights' differ from other kinds of rights? The concept of 'rights' is closely connected to that of 'right'. Something is 'right' if it conforms with a standard of rightness. All societies have standards of right, but it is often said that many cultures have no conception of people 'having rights'. The idea of everyone having 'human rights' is said to be especially alien to most cultures. Alasdair MacIntyre has argued that human rights do not exist. Belief in human rights, he says, is like belief in witches and unicorns, that is to say, it is superstition (MacIntyre 1981: 67).

MacIntyre's mistake is to think of 'human rights' as 'things' that we could 'have' as we have arms and legs. This mistake is embedded in the language of rights, for we do speak of our 'having' rights as we have mobile phones. Rights are, however, not mysterious *things* that have the puzzling quality of not existing, but *just claims* or *entitlements* that derive from moral and/or legal rules. This conception of rights defeats MacIntyre's objection that belief in human rights is superstitious, for there is nothing superstitious in thinking about what human beings may be entitled to. The justification of human rights requires a *theory* of human rights. We will examine theories of human rights in chapter 4. There we shall see that the problem of *validating* the concept of human rights lies partly in the general problem of validating beliefs, and does not arise only from supposed defects in the concept of human rights.

The social sciences

Social scientists neglected human rights until recently. The aspiration to be 'scientific' marginalized the legal and moral conceptions of human rights. However, the increasing importance of the concept of human rights in national and international politics has stimulated the interest of some social scientists. The explanation of variations in respect for human rights in different societies has been accepted as a proper object of social-scientific investigation. It is sometimes said that gross human-rights violations – such as genocidal massacres – are 'irrational' and beyond scientific explanation, but there is a body of knowledge about state behaviour, bureaucracy and ethnic conflict that may explain a great deal about such actions. There is much controversy about theories and methodology in the social sciences, but there is no reason why behaviour that violates or respects human rights should be less explicable than other complex social phenomena.

The academic study of human rights has been dominated by lawyers. This may be explained by the fact that the concept has been developed to a large extent through national and international law. The field of human rights has become a technical, legal discourse, and lawyers dominate it because they are the technical experts. Law appears to provide 'objective' standards that 'protect' the concept of human rights from moral controversy. This appearance is, however, illusory, for the meaning and application of human-rights standards is politically very controversial. International human-rights law is made by governments that act from political motives, and the extent to which it is implemented by those governments is influenced by political factors. Non-governmental organizations (NGOs), which have come to play an increasingly important role in the making of human-rights law, monitoring its implementation and campaigning for improved human-rights performance by governments, are political actors, even if they appeal to legal standards. Recent dramatic changes in the human-rights situations in the communist societies of Central and Eastern Europe, in Latin America, South Africa and elsewhere, have been primarily political events (Forsythe 1989; Donnelly 1998).

The study of international politics has been dominated by the theory of realism, which is concerned with the interests and power of states, and not with such ethical issues as human rights. The academic discipline of international relations has recently shown some interest in human rights (Dunne and Wheeler 1999; Forsythe 2000), but the topic remains marginal. Some international-relations scholars challenge the realist school by emphasizing the role in international politics of ideas in general, and of human-rights ideas in particular (Risse, Ropp and Sikkink 1999). The study of human rights in international politics has, however, with a few notable exceptions, fallen between international law, which is not systematically empirical, and international relations, which has neglected human rights for the supposed 'realities' of state power.

The neglect of human rights by the social sciences and the domination of human-rights studies by lawyers distort the concept of human rights. In the classic theory of 'natural rights' developed by John Locke in the seventeenth century every human being had certain rights that derived from their nature, and not from their government or its laws, and the legitimacy of government rested on the respect that it accorded to these rights (Locke [1689] 1970). The modern concept of human rights is a reformulation of this idea, and refers primarily to the relations between governments and their citizens. Political theory is the discipline that explains and evaluates these relations. Political science is the discipline that describes and explains the variations in the degree to which governments respect their citizens' rights. The contribution of political science to the study of human rights has, however, been disappointing. The study of human-rights issues has sometimes been carried out with the use of related concepts such as 'dictatorship', 'totalitarianism', 'authoritarianism', 'repression', 'state terror' and 'genocide'. There is also much work in political science on democracy that is relevant to understanding the current state of human rights. The desire of political scientists to be 'scientific', however, has led them to neglect a concept that appears at worst moralistic and at best legalistic.

The Western tradition of political theory has produced many formidable critics of such rights (Waldron 1987). This presents a strong challenge to the political science of human rights, especially since the classical critics are echoed by contemporary theorists (Brown 1999). Underlying any social sciences of human rights, therefore, are a number of controversial philosophical assumptions. This does not, however, distinguish the social science of human rights from other branches of social science, such as the politics of democracy or the sociology of inequality. Nevertheless, it requires the social scientist of human rights to be aware of these philosophical controversies.

Sociologists and anthropologists have recently begun to contribute to human-rights studies (Woodiwiss 1998; Wilson 1997c). The impact of the global economy on the protection of human rights has become an increasing subject of study (Evans 1998; 2001). This has been accompanied by an interest in 'the human-rights movement' as a transnational social movement (Risse, Ropp and Sikkink 1999). There are, therefore, signs that the social science of human rights is beginning to wake up.

Beyond human rights law

International law was traditionally concerned with regulating the relations among states with the primary aim of maintaining international peace. The leading concept of this project was that of *state sovereignty*, which forbade states from interfering with each other's internal affairs. The UN introduced the concept of human rights into international law without altering the concept of sovereignty. This legal framework is, however, subject to intense political pressures, as states and other actors seek to realize their interests and their principles in the international arena. The implementation of human rights by the UN is therefore highly politicized, and this leads to selective attention to human-rights problems, political bargaining and delays. The UN is not a utopian realm above politics, and the political character of human-rights implementation is unavoidable. The politics of human rights is not, however, always harmful to human rights, for governments may raise genuine human-rights issues from political motives, and, when political motives lead to a narrow and selective concern for human rights, appeals are sometimes made to human-rights principles that can be applied more widely.

The implementation of the UN's human-rights principles was seriously delayed and distorted for many years by the politics of the cold war. The UN proclaimed human rights, but did little to implement them. The cost of proclaiming human rights is low, and many governments, in the conditions of the cold war, thought that they had much to lose by respecting the human rights of their sometimes highly discontented citizens. In this context, what is at first sight surprising is the development, albeit slow, of international human-rights law, and of a movement of NGOs to campaign for its implementation. In this situation, the UN stood in an ambiguous position. On the one hand, it was the author and guardian of international human-rights standards; on the other hand, it was an association of governments that were often serious human-rights violators. The UN has, therefore, been the central institution where international human-rights law and politics meet, and often clash, and where the gap between human-rights ideals and realities is especially apparent.

The political character of human rights has philosophical implications. The lawyers who dominate human-rights studies sometimes rely, explicitly or implicitly, on the philosophy of *legal positivism*, which says that human rights are what human-rights law says they are. Human rights are, however, made and interpreted by a political process. The provisions of the Universal Declaration were the subject of intense debates, and the final text was produced by a long series of votes (Morsink 1999a). It is *politically* important that human rights have been codified in international and national law, but it is a mistake to believe that the legalization of human rights takes the concept out of politics.

The legal-positivist approach to human rights not only misrepresents their character, it also has dangerous implications. The *point* of human rights has historically been to criticize legal authorities and laws that violate human rights. Legal positivists sometimes say that the only rights are those that are legally *enforceable*. It may be desirable that human rights should be legally enforceable, but it is not necessary that they should be so. The concept of human rights implies that they are often not. If human rights were legally enforceable, one could, and normally would, appeal to one's *legal* rights, and would not need to appeal to one's human rights. One appeals to human rights precisely when legal institutions fail to recognize and enforce them. If legal positivism were true, an important basis for criticizing unjust legal systems would be eliminated.

The principal philosophical problem of human rights is to show how they can be justified, if they derive neither from law nor from superstitious beliefs. There is a historical reason why there is a problem about the 'source' of human rights. The first version of human-rights theory, presented by John Locke, assumed that God was the source of human rights. Locke could assume agreement with and among his readers that this source provided the ultimate validation of such rights: God was the source both of what exists and of value. The problem faced by the United Nations in proclaiming its Universal Declaration of Human Rights was that, precisely because it claimed that these rights were universal, it could not base them on any particular religious belief. The justificatory basis of human rights had to be *abstracted* from particular religious and ideological beliefs, but the character of that abstraction was not clear. The declaration says little about the source of these rights, apart from some large and unsubstantiated claims in the preamble that recognition of human rights is 'the foundation of freedom, justice and peace in the world', and that disregard for human rights has resulted in 'barbarous acts which have outraged the conscience of mankind'. These claims may contain important truths, but they do not give a clear account of the source of human rights.

The idea of the 'source' of human rights contains an important and confusing ambiguity. It can refer to the *social origins* or the *ethical justification* of human rights. Social scientists have studied the social origins of rights in, for example, popular political protest, and, important though such studies may be for a historical understanding of the discourse of rights, we must be careful not to confuse social origins with ethical justifications, since there are social origins of evil as well as of good. The social-scientific approach to rights, by its preference for avoiding ethical questions, sometimes falls into this confusion. There are, therefore, two distinct questions about the sources of human rights that we need to answer. Why *do* we have human rights? Why *should* we have human rights?

Another set of philosophical questions concerns the relations between human rights and other values. Do human rights occupy the whole space of moral and political theory, or are there other important values? If there are other important values, how are human rights related to them? The Universal Declaration claims that human rights are the foundation of freedom, justice and peace, but does not say how these values are related, conceptually or empirically. It is important to determine as clearly as possible the *limits* as well as the *value* of human rights. It is common to say that human rights establish *minimum standards* of good government. Claiming too much for human rights may make it harder to defend them against their critics, and thereby weaken their appeal and effects. We need to be clear, therefore, whether the concept of human rights supports a *comprehensive* or a *minimum-standards* political philosophy.

There is a huge gap between the fate of Lal Jamilla Mandokhel and the world of the United Nations – a gap that has been filled to a large extent by law and legal studies. These studies are certainly important. But the gap is also filled by politics, and by social, cultural and economic forces. These may be more important, although they have been relatively neglected in academic discourse. The aim of this book is to make a contribution to rectifying this neglect.

Conclusion

The study and, to a considerable extent, the practice of human rights have been dominated by lawyers. The cause of human rights owes a great debt to them. There is a danger, however, that excessive attention to human-rights law distorts our understanding of human rights. This book seeks to put law in its place by adopting an interdisciplinary approach. The concept of human rights has a history marked by philosophical controversies. Knowing that history and understanding those controversies illuminate the state of human rights today. In the past half-century, the concept has been incorporated into a large body of international and national law, but it has also been at the heart of political conflicts. The law is important, but understanding human rights requires us to understand its politics. Law and politics do not exhaust the human-rights field. The other social sciences – such as sociology, anthropology and economics – are essential to our appreciation of human-rights problems and their possible solutions. Human rights is an interdisciplinary concept *par excellence*.

We begin this inquiry by tracing, in chapter 2, the historical emergence of human rights. The story continues in chapter 3 by examining its gradual acceptance by the international community. Chapter 4 investigates the principal theoretical justifications of, and debates about, the concept. The distinctive contribution of the social sciences is then surveyed in chapter 5. In chapter 6, much-debated questions about the supposed universality of human rights and its relation to actual human differences are addressed, with particular emphasis on cultural minorities, indigenous peoples and the rights of women. In chapter 7 the place of human rights in national and international politics is analysed and the respective roles of international institutions, governments and non-governmental organizations evaluated. The political economy of human rights forms the subject of chapter 8, with special attention to development, globalization and international financial institutions. We conclude, in chapter 9, with reflections on the history of human rights, their current status and their likely future. One of the few certainties is that understanding human rights will be essential to understanding the world that we live in for a long time to come.

2
Origins: the Rise and Fall of Natural Rights

Why history?

The history of human rights can be studied for its own sake and for the sake of the light that it throws on the contemporary concept of human rights. Before we can study the history of human rights, however, we have to know what it is the history of. According to one view, the concept of human rights had little history before the establishment of the United Nations in 1945. On this view, the history of human rights would be the history of the UN concept. A more common view is that the contemporary conception of human rights has a much longer history. This view is better, because it enables us to investigate the historical and philosophical bases of the modern concept. It is, however, beset by controversy.

Some argue that the concept of human rights has a *universal* history in the various religions and philosophies of the world (UNESCO 1949; Chun 2001: 21), while others maintain that it originated in the West and was universalized only recently. Some argue that, if the *history* of the concept is Western, its *validity* cannot be universal. Others say that the history of a concept is irrelevant to its validity: there may be good reasons for universalizing a concept that has a particular history. Yet the validity of a concept depends on its meaning, and the meaning of the concept of human rights derives in part from how it has been used *historically*.

The most common view is that the concept of human rights originated in the West. Donnelly argues that, although non-Western cultures have important ethical concepts, they have traditionally lacked the concept of human rights (Donnelly 1989: part II). There is disagreement, however, about the history of the concept in the West. MacIntyre, for example, claims that, before about 1400, there is no expression in any language correctly translated by our expression 'a right'. He doubts whether human beings could have had rights if they could not have expressed them in their language (MacIntyre 1981: 66–7). Others argue that the concept of rights was implicit in ancient cultures. Tierney, for example, suggests that the commandment 'Thou shalt not steal' implies a right to property (Tierney 1988: 20–1). This controversy also has implications for the validity of the concept of human rights. MacIntyre suggests that the supposed fact that there was no concept of 'rights' before 1400 means that the concept of *universal* human rights is invalid.

Some scholars have argued that classical Greek thinkers could not think of individuals as having rights against the state because they believed that citizens were subordinate parts of the social whole. This idea, some say, was undermined by increasing social complexity which produced the concept of 'individuals', involved in various social relations, lacking definite social norms, and consequently having to create their own identities. The modern, complex society was, therefore, the precondition for the emergence of the concept of individual rights (Holmes 1979). This historical sociology of the concept of individual rights is thus supposed to undermine the concept of universal human rights. But is this history true?

On rights and tyrants

The contemporary concept of human rights is intended to protect individuals from the abuse of power by governments. Whether or not the ancient Greeks had a concept of rights, they certainly had the concepts of power and its abuse. This was expressed in the concept of tyranny, which was a form of government in which the ruler governed in his own interest and treated his people oppressively and unjustly. The concept of tyranny may imply that the rights of the citizen are being violated, but it was possible for the Greeks to think about tyranny without talking about rights. In Sophocles' play *Antigone*, for example, the king forbids Antigone to bury her dead brother because he had been a rebel against the state. Antigone defies the king's order, but on the ground that she has a religious *duty* to bury her brother, not on the ground that she has a *right* to do so. We might see this as a human-rights issue concerning freedom of religious practice, but Sophocles does not express it this way.

There are reasons, however, for rejecting MacIntyre's view that the ancient Greeks had no language of rights. Aristotle had a conception of rights and a language in which to express it. Aristotle believed that constitutions could assign rights to citizens. Citizens' rights included rights to property and to participation in public affairs. When these rights were violated, the laws determined compensation or punishment. Citizens' rights would be distributed differently in different political systems, for example in oligarchy and democracy. There is a range of expressions in Aristotle that we can properly translate as 'a right'. In particular, Aristotle used the expression *to dikaion* to mean a just claim, which we could translate as a right. Aristotle had no conception of *human* rights, however, as he believed that rights derived from constitutions, and that some men were slaves by nature (Miller, F. 1995).

Justice and rights

Roman law, through its influence on medieval ideas, provides the main link between classical Greek thought about rights and modern conceptions. The French historian Michel Villey initiated a debate on the distinction between *objective right* (that which is right) and *subjective rights* (personal entitlements). Villey argued that Roman law had no conception of subjective rights: the Latin word *ius* referred to objective right (Tuck 1979: 7–9; Tierney 1988: 4–6, 15). This view has been questioned on the ground that Roman law conceived of justice as rendering to each his right (*suum ius*) (Zuckert 1989: 74–5, 82). Whether *ius* was objective or subjective, it was *legal*, and not *natural* (Tuck 1979). The Stoic philosophers held that there was a natural law that was binding on all human beings, but they had no concept of natural rights. The Romans, therefore, like the Greeks, had no concept of universal human rights.

A clear shift from objective right to subjective rights took place only in the late Middle Ages, but how this occurred remains controversial. According to Tierney, medieval people had the concept of rights, and a language in which to express it, at least as early as the twelfth century (Tierney 1989: 626, 629). These rights were rights of particular persons, statuses, collectivities or classes. They were not natural rights. However, according to one conception of natural law, the right of nature was what was permitted by the law of nature. The rights of nature might be rights of individuals, but they were derived not from the nature of the individual but from the right order of society (Tierney 1989). The thirteenth-century writer Henry of Ghent held that each person had a natural right to self-preservation and property in his own body. This shows, Tierney argues, that the standard view, according to which the language of natural rights was a response to the emergence of complex, modern societies in the seventeenth century, is mistaken (Tierney 1992: 63–7).

The Magna Carta (1215) recognizes 'subjective' rights by such terms as 'his right' (*jus suum*) (Holt 1965: 96, 100, 104). The concept of rights was, however, at that time embedded in customary law. The Magna Carta was, further, not a summary of English law, but a text produced by specific political circumstances, and its purpose was to provide legal remedies for specific grievances. It was, therefore, not a charter of the rights of Englishmen, still less of human rights. Yet its reputation as a precursor of modern human-rights texts is not wholly unmerited. Article 39, for example, says that no free man shall be arrested, imprisoned, expropriated, exiled or in any way ruined, except by the lawful judgement of his peers or by the law of the land (Roshwald 1959: 361–4; Holt 1965:

1–2, 327). The Magna Carta emphasized property rights, but not only such rights, and it extended substantial rights beyond the baronial class. It was later transformed from a limited political and legal agreement into a national myth, and in the seventeenth century it was invoked as part of early modern debates about rights in England (Holt 1965).

One source of late medieval natural-rights theory was the dispute between the Dominicans and the Franciscans, who championed the life of poverty, and thereby called into question the legitimacy of private property. In 1329 Pope John XXII argued against the Franciscans that God had granted to Adam *dominium* (lordship) over temporal things. Property was therefore sanctified by divine law. By the fourteenth century it was possible to argue that to have a right was to be the lord of one's moral world (Tuck 1979).

Natural rights

There is no direct line from medieval conceptions of *ius* to early modern conceptions of natural rights. The humanist lawyers of the Renaissance, for example, were concerned not with natural rights but with *civil* rights (Tuck 1979). By the beginning of the seventeenth century there were two principal traditions of thinking about rights. The first emphasized natural, subjective, individual rights and the second emphasized objective right and/or civil rights (Tuck 1979: 54–7; Tierney 1989: 621).

The Dutch jurist Hugo Grotius was a crucial figure in transforming medieval ideas into the modern concept of rights. He began with the proposition that the will of God was law, and was known through man's sociability, which was the basis of all other laws of nature. Men had natural rights, but these were transformed by society. He conceived of *ius* both as what is just and as the ability of a person to have or do something justly. The law of nature concerned the maintenance of rights, the subject-matter of justice. 'Rights', Tuck says in his discussion of Grotius' ideas, 'have come to usurp the whole of natural law theory, for the law of nature is simply, respect one another's rights.' Everyone should enjoy his rights with the help of the community, which was required to defend our lives, limbs, liberties and property. Grotius held that moral obligations were owed not only to members of one's own society, but to mankind as such. He also maintained that his theory of natural law did not logically require belief in the existence of God, providing thereby the basis for a secular theory of natural rights (Tuck 1979; Tierney 1989: 621–2).

In seventeenth-century England Thomas Hobbes drew a sharp distinction between right (*jus*) and law (*lex*). Since right was liberty, and law was restraint, right and law not only differed from each other but were also opposites. In the natural condition of mankind, everyone had the natural right to do anything that was conducive to their preservation. There was both an obligation under the law of nature and a natural right to preserve oneself. The natural condition of mankind was one of war of each against everyone else, and therefore one of great insecurity. Reason required men to authorize a sovereign to act on their behalf. All men were obliged to obey this sovereign, provided that he did not threaten their preservation (Tuck 1979: 126–31).

We are so familiar with the use of the concept of human rights to limit the powers of government that we may be surprised to learn that most early modern natural-rights theorists argued that rational individuals would give up their natural rights to absolute rulers for the sake of social order. However, in 1642 Henry Parker argued that everyone had a property in himself and a natural right to self-preservation which could not be surrendered to government. In 1644 William Ball said that the basic rights of the people of England could be pleaded against any government. Should the government violate such rights, they would be in breach of trust, and the people might defend their rights by arms if necessary. The law of nature permitted them to defend their liberties and properties, which no civil law could nullify (Tuck 1979: 144–8).

In the English Civil War the Levellers adopted the concept of individual, inalienable rights and maintained that Parliament was violating them. Richard Overton argued that all governments were trusts, because by nature everyone had a 'self propriety' which could not be invaded or usurped without his consent. By 'natural birth' all men were equally born to such propriety and freedom. The concept of 'self propriety' entailed freedom of conscience, equal rights in law, and the right of at least the majority of men to vote. John Wildman thought that the concept of natural rights entailed the principle of universal suffrage. The Levellers held that persons were prior to estates, which justified the right to subsistence and the legitimation of some redistribution of wealth (Tuck 1979: 148–50; McNally 1989: 35–7; Roshwald 1959: 369; Ashcraft 1986: 155, 160–1, 163).

By grounding rights in the law of nature, the Levellers emancipated such claims from historical precedents. Richard Overton maintained that reason had no precedent, for reason was the fountain of all just precedents. Laws and governments come and go, but right reason endures for ever. Arguments from reason were, however, mixed with arguments from history, including references to the Magna Carta. This mixture of natural-law and historical argument created some ambiguity as to whether the rights claimed were those of Englishmen or universal human rights. Roshwald suggests that their practical emphasis was on the rights of Englishmen, but their logic was universalistic (Roshwald 1959: 366–70).

The deep ground for opposition to political absolutism in seventeenth-century England was the Protestant belief that God had made human beings rational so that each could determine their own way to salvation. The Protestant conception of reason entailed freedom of the will, the legitimacy of independent action and dissent from authority. Religion, on this view, required conscientious action that could oppose the individual to authority. This argument claimed to be based on what was common to all men and represented rational individuals as having been created in a state of equality and freedom. No one was, therefore, subject to the absolute will of any other person. These individuals constituted a natural moral community, since they lived under a framework of moral obligations that were owed to each other and to God. By the use of their reason, they were able to discover these obligations contained in the law of nature. This law not only imposed duties but also accorded rights to individuals, including, especially, the right to follow the dictates of one's conscience (Ashcraft 1986: 49, 66–7).

In his *Essay on Toleration* John Locke argued that man was a rational and active creature. Religious faith, therefore, must be active, and required liberty of action. The political authorities ought not to interfere with religious beliefs, since they concerned only the relation between the individual and God. The individual had a natural right to freedom of religion, both because salvation was infinitely more important than any political relation, and because political authorities were fallible in matters of religion (Ashcraft 1986: 88, 93–6).

Locke held that each individual had a responsibility to God to observe the law of nature. Every man was rational in that he could know the law of nature. God willed the preservation of mankind, and this imposed on everyone the obligation not to harm the lives, health, liberty and possessions of others. In 'the state of nature', in the absence of government, everyone had the right to self-defence and to enforce the laws of nature. Since everyone was judge in their own cause, they would be partial to themselves, and this would lead to conflict. Rational individuals would therefore agree to live under a government that was entrusted to enforce the law of nature and protect the natural rights of all through the rule of law, and to promote the public good. Governments that breached this trust, and that systematically and persistently violated the rights of the people, were tyrannies, lost authority to rule, and might be resisted by the people by force if necessary (Locke [1689] 1970). Locke is usually interpreted as a theorist of a strictly *individualist* conception of natural rights. This interpretation is supported by Locke's belief that each individual had fundamental obligations to God, was endowed with reason, and had a natural right to freedom, which was limited only by the obligation to respect the natural rights of others. Nevertheless, he also held that God's will for mankind could be achieved, and the natural rights of men could be protected, only in a political community, and that this community should be governed for the public good. There is, therefore, an unresolved tension in Locke's political theory between the natural rights of individuals and the collective good of society. The foundation of Locke's theory in the will of God and the reason of Man supported his belief that individual rights and public good were mutually compatible.

Locke argued that each individual had a property in himself, in his labour and in the products of his labour. Labour
was the basis of the right to private property. Locke's theory
of property has been the subject of prolonged controversy.
C. B. Macpherson interpreted Locke as a defender of 'possessive individualism' and of the interests of the bourgeois
class (Macpherson 1962). Critics have pointed out that
Locke's theory of rights was set in a Christian natural-law
framework, and that property rights were subject to a set of
moral obligations designed to provide for the common good
and the benefit of mankind. Locke's theory of property clearly
allows considerable inequality of wealth, but accords to
everyone the natural right to subsistence, and imposes on
those who have excessive wealth the obligation to aid those
who cannot meet their subsistence needs by their own efforts
(Ashcraft 1986).

The interpretation of Locke's theory influences our understanding of the history of human rights. Donnelly, for
example, repeats the common view that the modern conception of human rights derives principally from seventeenth-
century England and, in particular, from Locke's *Second
Treatise of Government*. The limits of Locke's theory, according to Donnelly, arise largely from the limited aims of 'the
bourgeois political revolution' (Donnelly 1989: 89, 104–5).
There is no historical basis, however, for the view that Locke
was seeking to justify or to assist a 'bourgeois political revolution' (Ashcraft 1986; McNally 1989). The contemporary
conception of human rights is a modification of Locke's
concept of natural rights, and it is therefore important to note
that Locke's concept was not simply 'bourgeois' in the way
that is sometimes suggested.

The age of revolutions

After the Glorious Revolution of 1689 the Lockean principles of constitutional monarchy and the rights to life,
liberty and property became part of Whig (liberal) ideology,
although the radical, egalitarian thrust of natural-rights
theory was muted. In the later eighteenth century, however,

radical Whigs appealed to the right of the people to reform or remove a government that did not protect their rights. The natural right to freedom of conscience was held to entail the principle that the state should not discriminate against anyone on the ground of religion, and that consequently everyone should be an equal citizen in a secular state. A few radicals, led by Mary Wollstonecraft, argued for the natural rights of women (Dickinson 1977).

The concept of natural rights was pervasive in eighteenth-century America. Americans linked the defence of religious liberty with the struggle for political freedom. American perceptions of the tendency of the British government towards tyranny and the fact that they were not represented in that government made it easier to justify resistance (Bailyn 1992; Dickinson 1977: 225). Although the influence of Locke on America is uncertain, the American Declaration of Independence (1776) certainly expressed Lockean ideas.

> We hold these truths to be self-evident, that all men are created equal, that they are endowed by their creator with certain unalienable rights, that among these are life, liberty and the pursuit of happiness – that to secure these rights, governments are instituted among men, deriving their just powers from the consent of the governed. That whenever any form of government becomes destructive of these ends, it is the right of the people to alter or abolish it.

The Virginia Declaration of Rights, which predated the American declaration by a month, included specific liberties that were to be protected from state interference, among them the freedom of the press, the free exercise of religion and the right not to be deprived of freedom except by due process of law. In 1791 the Bill of Rights was enacted as a set of amendments to the US Constitution, and included rights to freedom of religion, the press, expression and assembly, protection against unreasonable search and seizure, the right not to incriminate oneself, and the right to due process of law. These rights were based on historical precedents, but were justified by appeal to natural rights grounded in the laws of God. Notwithstanding the reference to God, however, the Declaration of Independence almost secularized the concept of natural rights. The Americans were also strongly constitutionalist, believing that the constitution, with its separation of powers, was the foundation of liberty. The American conception of natural rights at the time of the revolution did not include the rights of women, and was generally considered compatible with the institution of slavery (Bailyn 1992; Becker 1966; Dickinson 1977; Waldron 1987).

The secularization of the concept of natural rights that gradually took place during the eighteenth century created an important philosophical problem. The principles of morality and politics had to be derived from nature by reason. Late eighteenth-century secular natural-rights thinkers assumed that this could be done, but their arguments were often weak. By far the most impressive attempt to construct a liberal moral philosophy in this period was that of Immanuel Kant, who tried to show that reason could justify a set of ethical and political principles based on the obligation to respect the dignity of other persons as rational and autonomous moral agents. Critics of natural rights, however, began to mock the fondness of their advocates for declarations as well as for their lack of arguments. Attempts to derive natural rights from a cross-cultural consensus were undermined by evidence that no such consensus existed (Waldron 1987: 14–17). In the late eighteenth century, therefore, the concept of natural rights enjoyed a practical triumph in the American Revolution but rested on insecure theoretical foundations.

When the French Revolution broke out in 1789, the newly formed National Assembly proclaimed the Declaration of the Rights of Man and the Citizen in order to lay down the principles upon which the new constitution of France was to be founded. The declaration stated that the preservation of the natural rights of man was the aim of every political association. These rights were those of liberty, property, security and resistance to oppression. It affirmed equality before the law, freedom from arbitrary arrest, the presumption of innocence, freedom of expression and religion, the general freedom to do anything that did not harm others, and the right to property. The rights that it declared were qualified repeatedly by restrictions and conditions and were made subject to the rule of law. This ambivalence between individual natural rights and the requirements of social order reflected deep ideological differences among the revolutionaries. Nevertheless, the

French declaration was expressed in more universalistic terms than its American predecessors because the intransigence of conservative forces in France made it more difficult to appeal to historical institutions (Waldron 1987: 26–8; Baker 1994: 192–3).

The French Declaration of Rights was an act of revolutionary power carried out in the name of the popular will. The revolutionary governments faced, of course, many practical problems that threatened the stability of the new order. However, the degeneration of the revolution from the Declaration of the Rights of Man to the reign of terror had theoretical as well as practical sources. In the face of serious practical challenges, the ideological mixture of individual natural rights, popular sovereignty and commitment to the public good was insufficient to protect any of these values.

The ideology of the French Revolution was expressed in egalitarian terms. The theoretical concept of equal rights had, however, to be implemented in a society in which various forms of inequality existed. Yet in two respects the French Revolution was more egalitarian than the American. The question of the rights of women was raised, only to be quickly suppressed, and slavery was abolished, only to be restored by Napoleon (Hunt, L. 1996).

Inspired by the French Revolution, English radicals adopted the concept of the Rights of Man in preference to the appeal to historic rights, as they were seeking reforms for which there were no historical precedents. No one sought to universalize the significance of the French Revolution more than Thomas Paine. The Rights of Man, he maintained, promised 'a new era to the human race' (Dagger 1989: 301). They were the rights that men had by virtue of their status as human beings. They owed nothing to society or the state. The state had value, and therefore claims on the obligations of citizens, only as an instrument for the protection of the natural rights of individuals. Paine's conception of natural rights was uncompromisingly individualist and universalist: the Rights of Man were the rights of everyone, everywhere, at all times (Paine [1791–2] 1988: 171; Roshwald 1959: 347, 375–8). Paine also believed that a free, commercial society, with its associated inequalities of wealth, could be combined with political democracy in a way that would secure both individual rights and the common good. His emphasis on individual reason as the basis of politics made him a more robust champion of popular sovereignty than Locke had been, although he never considered votes for women (Philp 1989; Dickinson 1977).

Paine argued that historic rights were indefensible because no moment in history had priority over others as the basis of rights. The origin of human rights could be only the divine creation of human beings. Equal rights were necessary to motivate everyone to fulfil his duties to others. A system of rights was necessarily also a system of duties, for, if we all have rights, we all have duties to respect the rights of others. Notwithstanding his reference to the divine origins of rights, Paine's theory of the Rights of Man was grounded in reason, which could support a purely secular conception of human rights (Paine [1791–2] 1988: 65–70, 114; Philp 1989).

Paine saw civil society as naturally co-operative and progressive, and the need for governmental regulation as limited. By contrast, the essence of the state was coercion. As civil society grew more complex and stronger, so it both needed protection from the depredations of the state and had the ability to secure it. Paine thought that the pursuit of self-interest was legitimate in civil society, but that it ought to be subordinated to the common good in the political realm. Paine, like Locke, accepted inequalities of wealth as legitimate if they were products of differential rationality and industry, but he was more concerned with the misery of poverty than Locke was. In *The Rights of Man* and *Agrarian Justice* he made proposals for a system of public welfare financed by progressive taxation. There is, however, a tension between Paine's view of property rights as social and his view that natural rights have priority over civil rights. Paine anticipated the social-democratic argument that public guarantees of minimal welfare, far from violating the natural rights of anyone, sustain the rights of all (Philp 1989: 68–72, 75–6, 83–91).

The decline of natural rights

At the end of the eighteenth century the concept of natural rights was opposed by conservatives because it was too egalitarian and subversive, and by some radicals because it endorsed too much inequality of wealth. It suffered philosophically from uncertain foundations once its theological basis had faded. The violence of the French Revolution seemed to confirm the fears of the conservatives. The revolution discredited the concept of natural rights in England, but did not hold back the movement for reform. Conservatives and reformers, therefore, sought alternatives to natural rights from different motives.

Edmund Burke did not reject the concept of natural rights completely. He recognized the natural rights to life, liberty, freedom of conscience, the fruits of one's labour, property, and equal justice under the law. Nevertheless, he considered the concept generally to be, at best, a useless metaphysical abstraction and, at worst, subversive of social order. Thus, the 'real rights of men' were social rather than natural rights. Burke distrusted all abstract theoretical ideas in the making of public policy, as he believed politics to be essentially a practical activity that involved the making of judgements in complex circumstances. The French revolutionary doctrine of the Rights of Man was dangerous because it was simplistic and dogmatic.

Although Burke subscribed to natural-law theory, he opposed the universalism of the natural-rights concept for its failure to take account of national and cultural diversity. This cultural relativism offered little to those who had to endure tyranny. Significantly, Burke appealed to the concept of natural rights when analysing what he regarded as intolerable tyrannies, such as the Protestant rule in Ireland (Waldron 1987: 83–94; Freeman 1980).

Jeremy Bentham rejected the concept of natural rights more thoroughly than Burke did. Bentham sought to establish law on a rational basis. This required the elimination of all concepts that were vague or fictitious, and the concept of natural rights was both. For Bentham the facts of pleasure and pain were the basis upon which rational laws could be built, and the object of ethics and politics was the greatest happiness of the greatest number, or the common good. Legal rights were valid insofar as they contributed to the common good. Natural rights were, however, dangerous nonsense, because they might make stable society impossible. Claims of natural rights were vague, and so they could not be objectively evaluated, and disputes over natural rights were therefore likely to be settled by violence. Bentham believed that this explained the co-existence in the French Revolution of the Rights of Man and violence. Moreover, no rights could be absolute, because one right-claim might conflict with another, but, if the scope of rights was limited, there must be clear criteria for limiting rights and resolving conflicts among rights-claims. The theory of natural rights could not give a clear account of the limits of rights, whereas the principle of utility, Bentham believed, could. The concept of natural rights consisted of hasty generalizations from partially valid principles. Both the appeal and the danger of the discourse of natural rights lay in its simple dogmatism, and its refusal to engage in the hard intellectual work of thinking through the consequences of implementing general principles in the complex circumstances of society. Particularly absurd, Bentham thought, was the assertion that everyone was equal in rights. Even natural-law theorists believed that children were not equal in rights to adults, and, in practice, they did not accept equal rights for women, blacks, the poor, and others. The principle of utility evaluated inequality by its contribution to the general good, and thereby avoided the absurdities of the natural-rights approach (Welch 1984: 193–4; Hart 1982: 82; Waldron 1987: 36, 38–9, 42–3).

For Bentham the only rights were legal rights. Natural rights were supposed to derive from natural law, but this was fictitious. Once natural rights had been detached from the concept of divine law, Bentham argued, they were based on nothing at all. The principle of utility was a factual, objective standard by which the goodness or badness of laws could be evaluated. The principle of utility should, therefore, be adopted, and that of natural rights should be rejected (Waldron 1987: 35–7, 40; Welch 1984: 137–8).

In the nineteenth century utilitarianism superseded the concept of natural rights as the theoretical basis of reform in both England and France. In France, as in England, the concepts of natural rights and utility had been thought to be mutually compatible. As the revolution progressed, there was support in France for the view that the concept of natural rights was anarchic. A group of philosophers known as the Idéologues sought to set aside the concept of the Rights of Man, and to show how society could be reconstructed on the basis of a science of the mind with the aim of promoting happiness. They were, however, never able to convert their psychological theories into a convincing political programme (Welch 1984).

In contrast with this psychological approach, French social science moved away from the concern with political power and natural rights to an interest in economics. Economic science would deliver where natural rights had failed (Welch 1984). Saint-Simon developed a proposal for the organization of industrial society on a scientific basis that assigned priority to the social and economic over the political, the collective over the individual, and the scientific over the philosophical. The intellectual world of liberal political philosophy was left behind. The Lockean theory of property *rights* was transformed into the search for the *laws* of material production. The Saint-Simonians concluded that utilitarianism under the conditions of industrialism required socialism. The cause of the poor, neglected by the natural-rights ideologists of the French Revolution, was now transformed by the organized working-class movement.

Karl Marx argued that the Rights of Man were the rights of egoistic man, separated from the community. The concept treated society as external to individuals and as a limit on their natural freedom. It purported to be universal, but in fact expressed the interests of the bourgeois class, and, by emphasizing the rights of individuals, concealed the structured inequalities of class-based societies. It assumed, further, that individuals were actual or potential enemies, which might be true under the conditions of bourgeois egoism and capitalist competition, but was neither natural nor universal. It treated the pre-social, autonomous individual as natural, and political life as merely the means to protect the supposedly natural rights. This bourgeois conception of rights ignored the fundamental importance of labour, production and wealth to human well-being. Human emancipation, therefore, would be socio-economic (Waldron 1987: 126–32; Dagger 1989: 302–3). Marx was unclear as to whether the communist society would need no concept of rights or eliminate the *bourgeois* concept of rights. This was to prove to be a serious defect in Marx's theory when the twentieth century witnessed the development of strong communist states with official Marxist ideologies and no commitment to individual rights. A neo-Lockean concern with the protection of individual rights from abuse of power by the state was to play an important role in the politics of actual communist societies.

In the nineteenth and early twentieth centuries the founding fathers of sociology – Marx, Weber and Durkheim – were impressed by the massive social changes introduced by modern industrial capitalism, and sought to understand the larger historical forces that had brought them about. Individuals and their supposed natural rights dropped out of the picture. They were all in a sense neo-Aristotelians, seeing society as a natural entity to be understood scientifically, and not as an artificial creation to be shaped by ethical principles. If the concept of rights appeared in such analyses at all, it did so not as a fundamental philosophical category to guide ethical and political action, but rather as an ideological construct to be explained by social science. Sociology superseded philosophy. The science of society replaced the rights of man. Rights survived in the US Constitution, and thinkers such as de Tocqueville, J. S. Mill and Weber worried about individual freedom in the age of large-scale, impersonal organization. However, utilitarianism generally replaced natural rights as the basis of movements for social reform (Waldron 1987: 17–18, 151–3). The working-class and socialist movements nevertheless played a vital role in the struggle for economic and social rights.

The concept of individual rights survived in the late nineteenth century, but rights were defended not as natural rights but as conducive to the common good, either on utilitarian or neo-Aristotelian grounds transmitted through the philosophy of Hegel (Dagger 1989: 303). Certain practical political questions – such as slavery, minorities and colonial rule – were sometimes discussed in the language of the rights of man, and some predecessors of modern human-rights nongovernmental organizations, such as the French Ligue des Droits de l'Homme, were set up (Waldron 1987: 154). However, when the Covenant of the League of Nations was adopted in 1919 at the end of the First World War, it made no mention of the rights of man. It took the horrors of Nazism to revive the concept of the Rights of Man as human rights.

3

After 1945: the New Age of Rights

The UN and the human-rights revival

Since the General Assembly of the United Nations proclaimed its Universal Declaration of Human Rights on 10 December 1948, the concept of human rights has become one of the most potent in contemporary politics. In historical perspective, this fact is astonishing. A concept not long ago discredited has made a remarkable revival, and a concept widely perceived as Western has become global. The period from the French Revolution to the Second World War was the dark age of the concept of human rights. We are now in its second age.

International concern with what we now call human-rights issues had been shown intermittently in modern history in the campaigns against the slave trade and slavery, and in those for humanitarian laws of war, the protection of minorities and the emancipation of women (Robertson and Merrills 1996: 15–23). An international treaty to abolish the slave trade was concluded in 1890, and a treaty to abolish slavery was drafted in 1926. International concern with human rights between the two world wars was limited mainly to some work of the International Labour Organization on workers' rights and certain provisions in the treaties of the League of Nations for the protection of minorities, although the latter applied only to a few countries (Donnelly 1989: 210; Thornberry 1991: 38–54). The immediate cause of the human-rights revival, however, was the growing knowledge of Nazi atrocities in the Second World War. The allied governments asserted in the declaration by the United Nations on 1 January 1942 that victory was essential 'to preserve human rights and justice' (Nickel 1987: 1; Morsink 1999a: 1). Neither utilitarianism nor scientific positivism – the two philosophies that had undermined the concept of natural rights in the nineteenth century – were well suited to explain the evil nature of Nazism. The language of human rights seemed much more appropriate.

After the war, the United Nations Organization was set up to establish a new world order in accordance with the principles upon which the war had been fought. Support for a strong human-rights commitment came mainly from smaller countries in Latin America, the West and the third world. Opposition came mainly from the great powers, especially the USA and the USSR. Partly as the result of determined lobbying by non-governmental organizations (NGOs), the UN's San Francisco conference of 1945 included a number of human-rights provisions in the UN Charter (Cassese 1992: 25–7; Alston 1992a: 126–7).

The preamble to the charter declares that one of the chief aims of the organization is 'to reaffirm faith in fundamental human rights, in the dignity and worth of the human person, in the equal rights of men and women and of nations large and small.' Article 1 states that one of the principal purposes of the UN is 'to achieve international co-operation . . . in promoting and encouraging respect for human rights and fundamental freedoms for all.' Article 55 provides that the UN shall promote 'universal respect for, and observance of, human rights and fundamental freedoms for all without distinction as to race, sex, language or religion.' Article 56 tells us that all members of the UN pledge themselves to take joint and separate action in co-operation with the UN for the achievement of the purposes set forth in Article 55. Article 68 required the Economic and Social Council to set up commissions for the promotion of human rights, and on this basis the council set up the Human Rights Commission that was to draft the Universal Declaration. Article 62 said that the council 'may make recommendations for the purpose of promoting respect for, and observance of, human rights', and this was the basis on which it recommended to the General Assembly that it adopt and proclaim the declaration (Robertson and Merrills 1996: 25–6; Morsink 1999a: 2–4).

These provisions were qualified by Article 2, paragraph 7, which says that nothing in the charter shall authorize the UN to intervene 'in matters which are essentially within the domestic jurisdiction of any state.' The question as to whether violations of human rights are such matters has been one of the most controversial in the law and politics of human rights. The persistent UN concern with apartheid in South Africa shows how Article 2 (7) is no barrier to international action if there is sufficient will and unity in the international community. The General Assembly has not been much inhibited by Article 2 (7) in discussing human-rights issues, and 2 (7) has not prevented the establishment of UN procedures to investigate human-rights violations, although it may have been a barrier to their effectiveness (Cassese 1992; Robertson and Merrills 1996: 31).

The Universal Declaration of Human Rights

Since the Universal Declaration of Human Rights is some-times treated as a quasi-sacred text by its supporters and as a clumsy piece of bad philosophy by its critics, it is worth noting how it was made. A Canadian lawyer, John Humphrey, produced a first draft, based on a compara-tive survey of national constitutions. The Human Rights Commission then held eighty-one meetings over almost two years. The commission approved the final draft almost un-animously. Then the General Assembly Third Committee on Social, Humanitarian, and Cultural Affairs held more than one hundred meetings between September and December 1948. In this process, 1233 individual votes were cast. The Third Committee adopted the declaration by a vote of twenty-nine to none with seven abstentions. The General Assembly adopted the declaration on 10 December 1948, with forty-eight states voting for, none against, and eight abstaining (six communist states, Saudi Arabia and South Africa). Thus, most UN members endorsed most of the declaration, but those states were mainly from Europe and North and Latin America, with a few states from Africa and Asia.

Some states that played leading roles in drafting and approving the declaration had colonial empires, and much of the world's population lived under colonial rule. Since the adoption of the declaration, UN membership has more than trebled, with new members coming overwhelmingly from Africa and Asia. This has raised the question as to the applicability of the declaration to these countries. In this connection, it is worth noting that even the 1948 UN included capitalist and socialist states, rich and poor countries (such as the USA and Ethiopia), and societies that were predominantly Christian, Muslim, Hindu and Buddhist. Nevertheless, the Western states, including those from Latin America, were dominant (Morsink 1999a; Cassese 1992).

It is important not to confuse the nature or motives of those responsible for the declaration with their reasons. The Universal Declaration was intended to prevent a repetition of atrocities of the kind that the Nazis had committed. This is expressed particularly in the second paragraph of the preamble, which states that 'disregard and contempt for human rights have resulted in barbarous acts which have outraged the conscience of mankind.' The Human Rights Commission, aware of the religious, philosophical and ideological diversity of UN members, displayed no interest in the philosophical foundations of human rights. Nevertheless, given that Nazism violated human rights in theory and practice, the adoption of the concept of human rights by the UN in opposition to Nazi ideology clearly implied the commitment to some kind of neo-Lockean political theory. The substitution of the term 'natural rights' by that of 'human rights' may have been to eliminate the controversial philosophical implications of grounding rights in nature (Morsink 1999a: 283, 294–6, 300–2). The declaration set aside the traditional, but controversial, foundation of natural rights, without putting any new foundation in its place. Its strategy was to seek agreement on *norms* (rules) without seeking agreement on fundamental values and beliefs (Nickel 1987: 9). The concept of human rights is, however, sufficiently similar to the Lockean concept of natural rights that it is located in the Western liberal tradition. This makes it doubly controversial: because it is Western, and because it is liberal. However influential the concept of human rights may be, and however appealing it may be to many people, it is philosophically ungrounded (Waldron 1987: 151, 166–209). The problem of 'grounding' *any* concept philosophically is notoriously difficult, and concepts may be morally and politically useful, even though they are philosophically controversial. The actions of those who heroically resisted the Nazis may have been philosophically ungrounded, but are no worse for that.

The declaration has a certain Western bias in its emphasis on rights rather than duties, on individual rather than collective rights, on civil and political rather than economic, social and cultural rights, and its lack of explicit concern with the problem of imperialism (Cassese 1992: 31). It did, however, include the economic and social rights – such as the rights to work, health and education – that had been won in several industrial countries in the nineteenth and early twentieth centuries.

The declaration was not intended to impose legal obligations on states but, rather, to set out goals for which states were expected to strive (Robertson and Merrills 1996: 28–9). It was, nonetheless, a historic document. It was the first declaration of moral and political principles that could make a *prima facie* plausible claim to universality (Morsink 1999a: 33). Locke's theory and the French revolutionary declaration may have been universal in principle, but the UN declaration was endorsed by political powers with global reach. Whatever its philosophical limitations, the declaration has had great legal and political influence. Before the Second World War there was almost no international law of human rights. There are now approximately 200 international legal human-rights instruments, of which sixty-five acknowledge the Universal Declaration as a source of authority. The declaration is also the source of an international movement, and of numerous national movements, of political activists who struggle against oppression, injustice and exploitation by reference to this document (Morsink 1999a: xi–xii, 20).

Article 1 announces that all human beings are born free and equal in dignity and rights. They are endowed with reason and conscience, and should act towards one another in a spirit of brotherhood. Notwithstanding the echoes of Locke and the French Revolution, this is not unreconstructed natural-rights theory, but a liberal riposte to Fascism (Morsink 1999a: 38). Article 2 says that everyone is entitled to all the rights and freedoms set forth in the declaration 'without distinction of any kind, such as race, colour, sex, language, religion, political or other opinion, national or social origin, property, birth or other status.' This is both an explicit statement of the egalitarian implications of the concept of human rights, about which classical natural-rights thinkers had been so evasive, and a direct rejection of Nazi racist ideology (Morsink 1999a: 39). Article 2 is elaborated by Article 7, which states that all are equal before the law and are entitled to equal protection of the law without any discrimination.

Articles 3–5 deal with what are sometimes called 'personal integrity rights'. Article 3 restates the classic rights to life, liberty and security of person. Article 4 forbids slavery, servitude and the slave trade. Article 5 forbids torture and 'cruel, inhuman or degrading treatment or punishment'. Torture is widely condemned in the contemporary world, and widely practised, but the interpretation of the phrase 'cruel, inhuman or degrading treatment or punishment' has proved to be controversial.

Articles 6–12 deal with legal rights. These provisions are not controversial in general, although their particular applications may be, but the balance between legal rights, on the one hand, and social and economic rights, on the other hand, has been criticized for being excessively influenced by the Western history of rights as legal protections for private individuals against the state rather than as positive contributions to the life of dignity.

Article 14 says that everyone has the right to seek and to enjoy in other countries asylum from persecution. This article was influenced by Nazi treatment of the Jews, but the right of asylum has become one of the most important and controversial of human rights in recent times, as gross violations of other human rights have generated massive refugee flows, and many countries that claim to be champions of human rights are reluctant to defend the Article 14 human rights of foreigners.

Article 16 states that men and women of full age have the right to marry and to found a family without any limitation due to race, nationality or religion. They are entitled to equal rights as to marriage, during marriage and at its dissolution. Marriage shall be entered into only with the free and full consent of the intending spouses. This is the liberal view of marriage, and was a reaction against Nazi racial marriage laws. However, since the family is often at the centre of religious ethics, considerable tension has developed between this liberal conception of marriage rights and others, especially those that endorse 'arranged' marriages. Article 16 (3) asserts that the family 'is the natural and fundamental group unit of society and is entitled to protection by society and the state.' This unusual example of a collective right in the declaration was understandable in the light of Nazi family policy. But families, like all collective bodies, can be violators of human rights, for example, through domestic violence against women and the abuse of children, so that Article 16 (3) is more problematic than it first seemed to be.

Historically, the concept of rights had been closely associated with that of property. The socialist movement that arose in the nineteenth century had made that association problematic. Article 17 of the declaration states that everyone has the right to own property alone and in association with others, and that no one shall be arbitrarily deprived of his property. This is a relatively weak right to property, and is compatible with a wide variety of property systems.

Article 18 says that everyone has the right to 'freedom of thought, conscience and religion' and 'to manifest his religion or belief in teaching, practice, worship and observance'. This has been, historically, one of the most fundamental liberal rights, but it carries the potential problem that some religions may not respect some of the other human rights, and thus there can be a conflict between Article 18 and the rights listed in the other articles. Similarly, Article 7, which proclaims equality before the law, includes the right to equal protection against incitement to discrimination. This might conflict with Article 19, which says that everyone has the right to freedom of expression. This gives rise to the question as to whether so-called hate speech – speech expressing hatred or contempt for specific groups – can be made illegal without violating the right to freedom of expression.

It is commonly said that the Universal Declaration was innovative in including economic and social rights, which are largely missing from earlier rights declarations. We saw in the last chapter, however, that the idea of economic rights is much older than it is usually thought to be. The right to subsistence emerged in late medieval Christian thought. In the nineteenth century the working-class movement demanded, and secured, a number of economic and social rights, although debates about these were not typically conducted in natural-rights terms. Before the Second World War, the International Labour Organization (ILO), established in 1919, worked for fair and humane conditions of labour. The ILO did not, however, apply the term 'human rights' to its work until after the Second World War. Only a few ILO conventions are officially classified as human-rights treaties. These deal with freedom of association, the right to organize trades unions, freedom from forced labour and freedom from discrimination in employment. In recent years the ILO has increasingly emphasized the importance of civil and political rights for the protection of labour rights. Some commentators have argued that all the ILO's work concerns human rights, for it seeks to implement the right to fair conditions of work that is included in the Universal Declaration (Leary 1992: 582–4).

Economic, social and cultural rights were anticipated by the UN Charter. Article 55 says that the UN shall promote higher standards of living, full employment, conditions of economic and social development, and international cultural co-operation to create the conditions of stability and well-being necessary for peaceful and friendly relations among nations. Economic, social and cultural rights were included in the declaration because they were thought to be necessary to prevent a resurgence of Fascism and to promote the goals of the UN. The recognition of these rights represented a marriage between the tradition of liberal rights and that of socialism.

Article 22 says that everyone has the right to the economic, social and cultural rights indispensable for his dignity and the free development of his personality, 'through national effort and international co-operation' and 'in accordance with the organization and resources of each state'. Article 25 states that everyone has the right to a standard of living adequate for the health and well-being of himself and of his family, including food, clothing, housing and medical care and necessary social services, and the right to security in the event of unemployment, sickness, disability, widowhood, old age or other lack of livelihood in circumstances beyond his control. Article 22 makes the realization of economic, social and cultural rights dependent on the resources of each state, whereas Article 25 does not. Critics of economic and social rights argue that many states lack the resources to implement these rights, and therefore they cannot have a duty to do so. It follows that there cannot be human rights to these resources. The inclusion of the right to 'periodic holidays with pay' in Article 24 is often ridiculed because it universalizes a right that is relevant only to limited social conditions. This shows the difficulty in distinguishing between *human* rights and other rights.

The League of Nations had had a minority-rights regime, but the UN decided not to include minority rights in the Universal Declaration, although it did set up a Sub-commission on the Protection of Minorities. The only concession in the Universal Declaration to minority concerns, apart from the prohibition of discrimination, was Article 27, which says that everyone has the right 'to participate in the cultural life of the community'. This is, however, ambiguous as to whether 'the community' is the national community or includes minority communities, and it is therefore not very helpful to minorities. The UN took up the question of cultural minorities later, especially in Article 27 of the International Covenant on Civil and Political Rights (1966) and the Minority Rights Declaration (1992). We shall see, in chapter 6, that the place of minority rights in the human-rights system remains very controversial.

It is commonly said that human rights are indivisible and interdependent. This claim must be analysed carefully, however. Human rights are obviously divisible in the sense that it is possible to respect one right without respecting all. They are also obviously not wholly interdependent in that one can be violated without violating all the others. It is possible, for example, to respect the right to housing while violating the right to freedom of expression. The declaration rights are, however, indivisible and interdependent in the sense that the declaration does not allow the violation of some rights for the sake of others, and some rights are conceptually linked to others – for example, the requirement of equality in articles 2 and 7 (Morsink 1999a). The main problem of indivisibility has arisen from the relation between civil and political rights, on the one hand, and economic, social and cultural rights, on the other, especially since these two sets of rights were embodied in two separate UN covenants in 1966. Both the UN itself, and human-rights NGOs, have, until recently, interpreted human rights as civil and political rights, and dealt with economic and social rights under the concept of 'development'. It is often said that the two kinds of rights are distinguished by the fact that civil and political rights are cheap (it costs nothing to refrain from torture) whereas economic and social rights, such as the right to health, are expensive. This is an oversimplification, however, since some civil rights, such as the right to a fair trial, are expensive, whereas some economic and social rights, such as the right to food, might sometimes be respected better by reducing governmental regulation, and thereby reducing the financial burden of respecting the right on the national economy. The conceptual and empirical relations among these rights are, in fact, complex, and we shall analyse this complexity further in chapter 4.

A common criticism of the concept of human rights is that it neglects to emphasize human *duties*, and this encourages selfishness and social conflict. Article 29, paragraph 1, of the Universal Declaration states that everyone 'has duties to the community in which alone the free and full development of his personality is possible.' Paragraph 2 allows the limitation of human rights in order to secure the rights of others and to meet 'the just requirements of morality, public order and the general welfare in a democratic society'. This article is extremely vague. The declaration is vulnerable to the objection that the concept of human rights undervalues the importance of duties. This objection can be overcome, but only with a careful argument. The declaration gives little help in developing such an argument.

The UN conception of human rights, as expressed in the Universal Declaration, gives rise to a dilemma. If this conception of human rights has a philosophical justification, this will almost certainly be controversial, since all philosophical theories of rights are controversial. However, if the concept of human rights has no philosophical justification, then its claim to have moral force is unfounded. The declaration itself evades this dilemma, implying that the concept of human rights is somehow above philosophical controversies. Some lawyers resolve the dilemma by use of legal positivism, saying that human-rights law is law, whatever its philosophical status. This resolution does not work, however, because the UN concept of human rights is pre-legal, in the tradition of natural rights. The UN Charter says that the UN was determined to 'reaffirm' faith in human rights. According to the implicit political theory of the UN, human-rights law *codifies* human rights, it is not their *source*. The Universal Declaration revives the concept of natural rights in modern dress, but the philosophical justification for its claims remains unclear.

Donnelly holds that the Universal Declaration entails a relatively specific set of institutions, namely, the liberal-democratic welfare state (Donnelly 1998: 155). This raises the question as to whether there can be a set of rights to such institutions, especially since they are controversial even in those societies in which they are relatively well established (Parekh 1999). This leads to the problem of 'cultural relativism', which we shall examine in chapter 6. The Universal Declaration is a manifesto, and not a philosophical treatise or a social policy for the world. It was written for a popular audience in relatively simple terms, and it is therefore necessarily oversimplified as a guide to policy-making (Morsink 1999a). The declaration should be judged by clarifying and evaluating its underlying principles, and by investigating its empirical impact. This is the task to which we now turn.

From theory to practice

The cold war

The Universal Declaration of Human Rights is only a declaration. It makes no provision for its implementation. It allocates rights to everyone. It says little about who is obliged to do what to ensure that these rights are respected. In 1948 the UN was committed to state sovereignty and human rights. It could not decide what was to be done if sovereign states violated human rights. At that time virtually all governments said that the declaration was not legally binding. No human-rights violations, except slavery, genocide and gross abuses of the rights of aliens, were illegal under international law. The UN established a Commission on Human Rights, but it was composed of the representatives of governments, and NGOs had limited access to it. The commission's mandate was confined largely to drafting treaties and other legal texts. In 1947 the Economic and Social Council declared that the commission had no authority to respond to human-rights violations in any way. A procedure was established to channel the thousands of complaints that the UN received each year, which the head of the organization's human-rights secretariat described as 'the world's most elaborate waste-paper basket' (Alston 1992a: 128–9, 140–1; 1994: 375–6; O'Donovan 1992: 117). From 1948 until the late 1960s the ability of the UN or the 'international community' to take effective action to protect human rights was extremely limited (O'Donovan 1992: 119; Alston 1992a: 139).

The cold war reinforced the reluctance of states after 1948 to submit to the international regulation of human rights, and, consequently, notwithstanding the Universal Declaration, human rights returned to the margins of international politics in the 1950s. The two main cold-war protagonists, the USA and the USSR, used the concept of human rights to score propaganda points off each other, while directly or indirectly participating in the gross violation of human rights. Plans to introduce binding human-rights treaties were delayed until the mid-1960s.

In the 1960s the world-wide decolonization movement created many new member-states of the UN, with new issues for the human-rights agenda: anti-racism, decolonization and the right to self-determination. The Convention on the Elimination of all Forms of Racial Discrimination was adopted by the General Assembly in 1965. The arrival of new states at the UN, therefore, injected a new activism, although it was very selective: South Africa, Israel and Chile received particular attention. As UN human-rights activism grew, so human-rights politics threatened the universality of the concept in practice.

Even this selective activism, however, advanced the cause of universalism, because it set precedents that were broadened later. For example, in 1965 the Special Committee on Decolonization asked the commission to respond to the petitions that the committee had received about the situation in southern Africa. The council then asked the commission to consider violations 'in all countries.' In 1966 the General Assembly asked the Economic and Social Council and the Commission on Human Rights 'to give urgent consideration to ways and means of improving the capacity of the United Nations to put a stop to violations of human rights wherever they might occur.' This led to the adoption of two new procedures. In 1967, Resolution 1235 of the Economic and Social Council authorized the commission to discuss human-rights violations in particular countries. In 1970 Resolution 1503 of the council established a procedure by which situations that appeared to reveal 'a consistent pattern of gross and reliably attested violations of human rights' could be pursued with the governments concerned in private. The post-colonial states had wanted the commission to deal with racism. The communist states thought that this would embarrass the West. The West did not want to appear to condone racism, but did not want racism to dominate international human-rights debates. Thus cold-war and third-world politics generated new procedures and wider powers for the UN Human Rights Commission.

The work of the commission under its 1235 powers was very selective in the 1970s. It was, for example, very concerned with South Africa, Israel's occupied territories, and Chile, but did not respond to gross human-rights violations in East Pakistan (now Bangladesh), Uganda, the Central African Empire, Cambodia, East Timor, Argentina, Uruguay, Brazil and many other places. In the 1980s the 1235 work of the commission broadened considerably. The commission has still been criticized for lack of political balance, but its scope is much wider than it was, and much wider than it could be before the adoption of 1235. Its response time is slow, and potential sanctions are remote. The 1235 procedure is an

advance in the implementation of UN human-rights standards, but it works unevenly and remains marginal to the
world's human-rights problems (Alston 1992a; Donnelly
1989: 208; 1998: 9; 1999: 76, 101).

The 1503 procedure enables individuals to petition the UN
about human-rights violations, but offers them no redress. The
commission names countries that it has considered, and may
therefore put some pressure on governments by publicity.
However, the procedure can be brought fully into effect only
at least two years after receipt of the complaint. Stalling tactics
by governments and the politics of the commission can delay
action much longer. 1503 has had little impact on situations
of gross human-rights violations (Robertson and Merrills
1996: 79–89; Donnelly 1998: 9, 53–4; Alston 1992a; Forsythe
1995: 306). There is a consensus that 1503 is slow, complex,
secret and vulnerable to political influence, and there is a
difference of view among experts as to whether it does more
harm than good (Alston 1992a: 150–5; Donnelly 1989: 208).

In 1966 two international treaties – the International
Covenant on Civil and Political Rights and the International
Covenant on Economic, Social and Cultural Rights – were
opened for signature and ratification. They entered into force
in 1976, when the necessary thirty-five ratifications had been
received. The 1966 covenants leave out the right to property,
but include the right to self-determination. The Universal
Declaration and the two covenants, together known as the
International Bill of Rights, constitute the core of international human-rights law. By August 2001 more than 140, or
slightly more than three-quarters of the 190 UN states, had
ratified the two covenants (Office of the United Nations High
Commissioner for Human Rights 2001).

The Human Rights Committee was established in 1976.
It consists of independent experts whose task is to monitor
compliance with the Covenant on Civil and Political Rights.
The states that are parties to the covenant are obliged to
submit reports on what they have done to implement the
rights in the covenant. The committee can also receive complaints from states under the covenant and complaints from
individuals under its optional protocol. NGOs have played
an increasing role as sources of information. The committee
has jurisdiction only over states that are parties to the

covenant, but most states are now parties. Co-operation with the committee by states is variable, but the committee has brought about legislative changes in some countries, and can contribute to human-rights improvements through discussion, debate and advice. In a few cases, individual complainants have benefited from a decision of the committee (Opsahl 1992; Robertson and Merrills 1996: 45–6, 66, 71; Donnelly 1989: 208–10; 1998: 57–9).

New initiatives to implement human rights were taken in the 1970s in the foreign policies of certain states. In 1975, US foreign aid policy was required to take account of the human-rights practices of recipient countries. When Jimmy Carter became president in 1977, he introduced human rights into his foreign policy. This was an innovation, although the policy was implemented unevenly in practice (Donnelly 1998: 10). Human-rights NGOs were making an increasing impact. Amnesty International, for example, was awarded the Nobel Peace Prize in the year in which Carter became president. The UN adopted the Convention on the Elimination of Discrimination against Women in 1979, the Convention against Torture in 1984, and the Convention on the Rights of the Child in 1989. New 'thematic' procedures evolved. A Working Group on Enforced or Involuntary Disappearances was established in 1980 in response to events in Argentina and Chile. A special rapporteur on summary or arbitrary executions was appointed in 1982. In 1985 a special rapporteur on torture was appointed. Other special rapporteurs have dealt with religious intolerance and human-rights violations by mercenaries, and a Working Group on Arbitrary Detention was set up in 1991. Almost all these thematic procedures apply only to civil and political rights, and not to economic and social rights. Special rapporteurs were appointed to study the human-rights situations in a growing number and increasingly diverse range of countries. By 1995 fourteen experts were reporting to the commission as special representatives or rapporteurs. These were procedural advances in the UN implementation of human rights, but they have been thinly staffed, poorly funded and not often successful in remedying human-rights violations. They remain marginal to the protection of human rights world-wide (Forsythe 1995: 304–5; Alston 1992a: 180–1).

Developments in the UN were overshadowed by the impact of the cold war, which was overwhelmingly adverse for human rights. The communist states were gross violators of human rights, and the Western powers, led by the USA, supported regimes around the world that committed grave human-rights violations. Ironically, the instability of the cold-war 'balance of power' created an opening for human-rights progress. In the early 1970s the communist bloc sought agreements with the West on security and economic matters. The West demanded human-rights guarantees in return. In 1973 the Conference on Security and Co-operation in Europe (CSCE) was convened, later to become the Organization for Security and Co-operation in Europe (OSCE). This led to the Helsinki Final Act of 1975, in which the communist states accepted a range of human-rights commitments. In the following years, Helsinki-based human-rights NGOs were established in the USSR, but were severely persecuted. In 1977 the human-rights group Charter 77 was set up in Czechoslovakia. The short-term, practical effects of these events appeared slight, but they increased the intensity of international debates about human rights, and such groups played a role in the dismantling of the communist system in Eastern Europe (Donnelly 1998: 78–82; Forsythe 2000: 124–5).

The admission to the UN of a large number of poor, non-Western states introduced a new emphasis on economic rights into international debate. In 1974 a number of texts concerning the so-called New International Economic Order were approved. These texts sought to draw attention away from human-rights violations in individual states to the structural causes of human-rights violations in global economic inequality. This third-world approach to human rights led to a controversial conceptual development: the so-called third generation of human rights. According to this new thinking, civil and political rights were the first generation of 'liberty' rights; economic and social rights were the second generation of 'equality' rights; and there was now a need for a third generation of 'solidarity' rights. These were the rights to development, peace, a healthy environment and self-determination. In 1986 the General Assembly adopted a Declaration on the Right to Development. Third-generation rights have been criticized on several grounds, including the following: (1) the language of 'generations' is inappropriate, because generations succeed each other but so-called generations of human rights do not; (2) the concept of 'generation' presupposes a questionable history of human rights: the supposed first two generations were both recognized in the Universal Declaration; (3) it is not clear whether the holders of these rights are individuals, peoples, states or some combination of these; (4) it is not clear to what the bearers of these rights have a right; (5) it is not clear who the corresponding duty-bearers are, or what their duties are; (6) these rights-claims provide cover for authoritarian governments to violate established human rights; and (7) what is valid in third-generation rights is already contained in established human rights: for example, the right to development is covered by taking economic and social rights seriously (Donnelly 1993; Freeman 1999: 34–6).

In the 1980s and early 1990s the theme of 'cultural relativism' became more salient in UN debates about human rights. In 1984 the Islamic Republic of Iran proposed that certain concepts in the Universal Declaration should be revised, and announced that Iran would not recognize the validity of any international principles that were contrary to Islam. In the run-up to the UN World Conference on Human Rights that was held in Vienna in 1993 there was much talk of a conflict between 'Asian values' and human rights. The final declaration of the Vienna conference reaffirmed the universality of human rights, but conceded that human rights 'must be considered in the context of a dynamic and evolving process of international norm-setting, bearing in mind the significance of national and regional particularities and various historical, cultural and religious backgrounds.'

After the cold war

Although the end of the cold war brought some immediate human-rights improvements, such as the establishment of civil and political rights in former communist societies, the new world order produced complex human-rights patterns.

Both the General Assembly and the Human Rights Commission became more active. The challenge to Western domination of the human-rights agenda by the poorer states of the so-called South weakened. The UN goals of peace-keeping and human-rights protection became increasingly combined. The Secretary-General's office negotiated a human-rights agreement between government and rebels in El Salvador, which involved intrusive monitoring by UN civil and military personnel. Similarly, in Haiti and Liberia, the UN became involved in monitoring respect for human rights as part of political settlements. In Namibia and Cambodia, the UN had a more comprehensive role in protecting human rights in the context of overall political reorganization. Initiatives by the Secretary-General or mandates from the Security Council provided bases for UN supervision of elections in Nicaragua, Haiti, El Salvador, Namibia, Angola, Cambodia and elsewhere. In 1991 Operation Desert Storm reversed the Iraqi military occupation of Kuwait, and was followed by military interventions in northern Iraq to create a 'safe haven' for the persecuted Kurds and in southern Iraq in an attempt to defend the Shi'a population. In the following year the UN intervened in the civil war in Somalia to end the fighting and provide humanitarian assistance. It was more successful in the latter operation than in the former, but the intervention was problematic for the UN, the intervening states, especially the USA, and the intended beneficiaries.

If the intervention in Somalia had only limited success, the wars in the former Yugoslavia provided an even more complex challenge. The dissolution of the former Yugoslavia left a Serb minority in Croatia, three minority populations in Bosnia-Herzegovina (Serbs, Croats and Muslims), and an oppressed ethnic Albanian minority in Kosovo. Serbia launched a war against Croatia, ostensibly to protect the Serb minority, and intervened in Bosnia on behalf of the Bosnian Serbs. The war in Bosnia involved 'ethnic cleansing' (forcible moving of populations in order to create ethnically homogeneous territories) and other gross human-rights violations, including massacres and mass rapes. The UN, and particularly the major powers, were reluctant to intervene militarily, partly because of their experience in Somalia and partly because of the perceived military and political difficulties.

Considerable success was achieved in delivering humanitarian assistance, but the UN's failure to prevent gross human-rights violations was catastrophic. In 1999 NATO intervened militarily in Yugoslavia, when the UN could not because of Russian and Chinese opposition in the Security Council, in order to prevent violations of the human rights of ethnic Albanians in Kosovo. The immediate effects were worse violations against the Albanians, considerable war casualties among Yugoslav (Serb) civilians, and, after the NATO military victory, reprisals by Albanians against Serbs. The brutal and corrupt regime of the Yugoslav President, Slobodan Milosevic, was overthrown, and Milosevic was arrested and charged with crimes against humanity, war crimes and genocide by the International Criminal Tribunal for the Former Yugoslavia (International Criminal Tribunal for the Former Yugoslavia 2001; Osborn 2001). The legality of the NATO intervention was dubious, and it was controversial, even among human-rights observers. Its outcome is uncertain, as is the future of interventions for the sake of human rights generally.

The establishment of international criminal tribunals for the former Yugoslavia and following the genocide in Rwanda were further innovations by the UN, which also agreed to set up a general international criminal tribunal. It remains to be seen whether this combination of law and politics is successful, or whether, as some critics fear, the law may undermine the chances of political settlement (Forsythe 1995: 313–14).

The UN has had for a long time a small and poorly funded programme of technical assistance for human rights, for example in legal institution-building. In the early 1990s this was somewhat expanded. Some observers prefer this constructive assistance for human rights to more adversarial pressure, while others believe that such programmes achieve little, and can divert attention from human-rights violations. The UN also acts to mitigate the effects of human-rights violations through the High Commissioner for Refugees (UNHCR). Although UNHCR does extremely valuable work, it acts typically after gross human-rights violations have taken place, and despite its efforts the problem of refugees is becoming worse, not better (Forsythe 1995: 307–9).

The Vienna conference of 1993 reaffirmed the universality, indivisibility and interdependence of human rights. It also emphasized the special vulnerability of certain groups – such as women, children, minorities, indigenous populations, handicapped persons, migrant workers and refugees – and opened the way for the appointment of a High Commissioner for Human Rights.

At the beginning of the twenty-first century, there is concern that 'globalization' is a threat to human rights. Concern for globalization has shifted the human-rights agenda somewhat in favour of economic and social rights, and has raised questions about the human-rights obligations of non-state actors, such as multinational corporations. Ironically, after the apparent victory of capitalism over communism, anti-capitalist protest has once again become part of international politics. Another human-rights problem associated with globalization is that of the increasing numbers of asylum-seekers and the reluctance of the governments into whose jurisdiction they flee to respect their rights in full.

Globalization is, however, an extremely complex process, and we shall examine its impact on human rights in chapter 8.

Conclusion

Since 1945 the UN has done a lot of 'standard-setting', institution-building and human-rights promotion. The concept of human rights is one of the most influential of our time, and many poor and oppressed people appeal to it in their quest for justice. The capacity of the UN to implement its own standards is still modest, however. The concept of state sovereignty and the realities of international power politics still make the implementation of human-rights standards uneven, and generally weak. There is widespread lip-service to human rights by governments, and also much hypocrisy. This may nevertheless have the advantage that human-rights violators can be shamed into making human-rights improvements. Lip-service may, however, be a substitute for action.

There is an important role for NGOs in converting lip-service into effective action.

It is difficult to evaluate the success of the UN human-rights project precisely. Its achievements have clearly been limited, but it may be that the combined effect of UN agencies, governmental policies and NGOs has improved the human-rights situations in many countries, although gross human-rights violations are still common. The failure of the UN to respond effectively to the situation in Rwanda, despite the fact that it received early warning of the genocide, shows that its limitations can still lead to disaster. The UN carried out a human-rights revolution in world politics, but it is a long revolution in its early stages, and success is not guaranteed. The international politics of human rights is part of international politics. This means that it is characterized by a considerable amount of self-interest, pragmatism and short-term crisis management, rather than systematic implementation of principles (Forsythe 1995: 309–10).

The UN has failed to prevent many human-rights catastrophes, and has also failed to sustain its own commitment to the indivisibility of human rights. Economic, social and cultural rights have been neglected in the main UN agencies, especially the General Assembly and the commission. The International Labour Organization (ILO) has done much work to convert general economic and social rights into relatively precise standards, and has attempted to integrate this standard-setting with technical assistance. Although the ILO specializes in social and economic rights, it takes indivisibility more seriously than the rest of the UN, and is conscious that civil and political rights are necessary for the protection of economic and social rights. The ILO is not free from the political disputes that pervade other UN bodies, but this is partly mitigated by the active participation of employers', workers' and other non-governmental organizations (Leary 1992; Donnelly 1998: 62–4). The ILO is, however, somewhat marginal in the UN human-rights system, and this may have limited its overall contribution to the improvement of human rights (Leary 1992: 619).

The International Covenant on Economic, Social and Cultural Rights was adopted by the UN in 1966, and came into effect in 1976. It was not until 1986, however, that the

UN established a Committee on Economic, Social and Cultural Rights to monitor compliance with the covenant. Alston has said that, in addition to the problems faced by all UN human-rights bodies, this committee has a number of peculiar difficulties: lack of conceptual clarity of many of the relevant norms; lack of enthusiasm of many governments for these rights; the ideological contentiousness of the rights; the absence of national institutions that recognize the rights; the complexity and scope of the information required to supervise compliance effectively; the more limited relevance of formal legal texts and judicial decisions; and the lack of NGOs with expertise on, and concern with, economic rights. The impact of the committee in these circumstances has been weak (Alston 1992b).

The UN human-rights system is a 'regime': that is, a set of norms and institutions that is accepted by states as binding. The UN human-rights regime is based on the Universal Declaration. The Vienna Declaration and the relatively large number of signatories to the 1966 covenants show that most states accept the legitimacy of this regime. Yet the concept of state sovereignty remains strong, and implementation of human-rights standards is uneven and sometimes disastrously ineffective. Since the end of the cold war there has been some attempt at human-rights enforcement, but this has proved uneven, not very effective, and to some extent counter-productive. That the regime is strong on declarations and weak on implementation and enforcement reflects the interests of the principal international actors: *states* (Donnelly 1989: 211–12). Nevertheless, the political character of international human-rights institutions can promote human rights if a sufficiently strong alliance of states exerts pressure on an offending state with an interest in conforming with the demands of the society of states. The international human-rights regime has some prestige in world politics that gives it the potential for mobilization. Its political selectivity undermines this prestige. The office of the High Commissioner for Human Rights is another instrument for impartial human-rights promotion and, perhaps, implementation (Donnelly 1998: 82–4).

The international human-rights regime is political, not philosophical. It responds pragmatically to circumstances, and consequently operates inconsistently. The relatively coherent ideals of the Universal Declaration are, therefore, in practice unevenly implemented. The UN is a club of states, represented by governmental leaders, and, notwithstanding their conflicts of interest and ideology, they have a common interest in mutual accommodation. This may inhibit robust action for human rights when such action might upset the diplomatic apple-cart. While the legal institutions of the UN may be more impartial, they are procedurally restricted and diplomatically cautious. The political organs have more freedom of action, but may be more selective.

We should not forget that the very existence of the international human-rights regime is astonishing. In the last chapter we saw that the concept of natural rights was discredited by the French Revolution and then overtaken by social science, and especially the political economy and sociology of industrial capitalism. In reaction against Nazism, the UN revived the natural-rights tradition by adopting the concept of human rights, and included in the new concept concerns with economic and social justice. Attempts to maintain the 'indivisibility' of human rights have, however, had very limited success. In the next chapter we shall explore some of the underlying theoretical problems.

On the foundation of the Universal Declaration an elaborate structure of global and regional human-rights treaties and declarations has been built. The regional regimes of Europe, America and Africa vary greatly in their effectiveness – the European being relatively strong, and the African very weak. In addition, there are, of course, human-rights provisions in the constitutions and laws of many states. Many of these are impressive on paper, but bear little relation to what happens in the streets and the fields.

The concept of human rights is a concept whose time has come. But what is it precisely that has come? How should we evaluate it in the light of (a) the criticisms that were made of its historical predecessors; and (b) its uneven record of success in practice? In the next chapter we shall examine theories of human rights that have attempted to clarify and justify the concept, and that have offered relatively precise answers to these questions.

4
Theories of Human Rights

Why theory?

The revival of human rights by the UN ignored the criticisms that had been made of the earlier concept of natural rights. Its practice of human-rights declarations, promotion, standard-setting and institution-building has been carried out by politicians and lawyers, prompted and assisted by activists. They have not been much concerned with the theoretical justification of this practice – indeed they may have considered theoretical justification unnecessary. Human-rights practice was addressed mainly to obvious human wrongs – such as racism, colonialism and political oppression – and it might be tempting to follow the American Declaration of Independence and to consider the truth of human rights to be 'self-evident'. This is quite unsatisfactory, however, because the concept of human rights is clearly controversial and in need of justification. The history of the concept shows why this is so.

Since the classical concept of natural rights had been based on Christian, natural-law theory, its secularization called its foundations into question. When the validity of the concept could no longer be guaranteed by the will of God, the Rights of Man were said to be derived from reason and/or nature. However, this derivation was very controversial. The critics of the Rights of Man – such as Burke, Bentham and Marx – could appeal to reason and nature in different ways in order to reject the concept. In the nineteenth century, 'reason' came to mean 'scientific reason', and science was hostile to the concept of natural rights. There was also a reaction against the individualism of natural-rights theory and a revival of the Aristotelian idea that society was the primary concept of political philosophy. Thus, *social science* was hostile to natural rights on two grounds: the concept was unscientific and it was anti-social. From the perspective of modern philosophy and social science, the UN revival of the concept was very problematic.

Scepticism about human-rights theory can be defended theoretically. Richard Rorty has argued that there is *no* theoretical foundation for human rights, because there is no theoretical *foundation* for any belief. This is not, however, something we should regret, both because it is a necessary philosophical truth, and because the cause of human rights does not require theory for its success, but, rather, sympathy (Rorty 1993). Rorty's argument, however, confuses *motivation* and *justification*. Sympathy is an emotion. Whether the action we take on the basis of our emotions is justified depends on the reasons for the action. Rorty wishes to eliminate unprovable metaphysical theories from philosophy, but in his critique of human-rights theory he goes too far, and eliminates reasoning. We need reasons to support our human-rights actions, both because it is often not clear which actions human-rights principles require and because opponents of human rights can support their opposition with reasons. We must understand whether our reasons are superior, and, if so, why.

A different kind of objection to human-rights theory has been put forward by the political scientist David Forsythe. He argues that philosophical theories are inherently controversial, and that concern with theory will undermine human-rights practice (Forsythe 1989). Forsythe is interested primarily in the politics of human-rights law. However, human-rights politics is influenced by its implicit theory, and the neglect of theory will lead to an inadequate understanding of the politics as well as an insufficient justification of the practice. Forsythe implicitly admits this when he says that, for many actors in world politics, the philosophy of human rights matters (Forsythe 1989: 60). Human-rights law presents the conclusions of certain arguments. Human-rights theory provides the arguments.

Burke, Bentham and Marx all believed, for different reasons, that declarations of rights such as that of the French Revolution should be severely criticized. Their arguments could be applied to the Universal Declaration of Human Rights. It would be irresponsible to assume dogmatically that such arguments are mistaken. Theoretical criticisms of rights declarations require a considered theoretical response. Practical agreements among those with different theories are certainly, as Forsythe maintains, desirable in international politics. However, if we wish to understand why such agreements are desirable, how they are possible, and why they are difficult to implement, we should examine the different theories that support or undermine the concept of human rights.

Forsythe suggests that human-rights law and practice should be evaluated, not by ideal standards, but by 'real possibilities' (Forsythe 1989: x). However, political theorists now commonly distinguish between 'ideal theory' and 'non-ideal theory'. Ideal theory does not describe reality, but puts forward reasoned argument for certain standards with which to evaluate reality. Non-ideal theory introduces reality, and thereby analyses 'real possibilities'. Ideal theory directs us to the 'real possibilities' that are *worth realizing*. Ideal theory is very practical, therefore. It endorses standards for evaluating practical reality and for guiding our actions. Reality may well limit the pursuit of the ideal quite strictly, but we cannot understand how it does so if we have no conception of the ideal.

Alan Gewirth has given the following arguments for human-rights theory. All claims of human rights assume that they are justified. However, the reasons for this belief are often not clear, and, if they are not clear, we cannot know whether or not they are good reasons. Also, different persons may make conflicting human-rights claims, and, without a theory of human rights, we cannot rationally choose between them. Human-rights theory seeks to answer questions such as the following. Are there any human rights? How do we know what they are? What is their content and scope? How are they related to each other? Are any of them absolute, or may they all be overridden in certain circumstances? (Gewirth 1981). We can give *legal* answers to these questions, but such answers only give rise to the further question as to whether the law is what it ought to be.

While the Universal Declaration was being drafted, UNESCO, the UN cultural organization, undertook an inquiry into the theoretical problems of such a declaration. In his introduction to the published results of this inquiry, Jacques Maritain described the project as a search for the philosophical bases of human rights, that is, the correct interpretation and justification of the concept. Maritain suggested that there was a need to provide a justification for the concept, but a consensus on the justification was impossible in view of the diversity of philosophies in the world. There could be agreement on what human rights there were, but not on why there were these rights. Practical agreement would be combined with theoretical disagreement. There must, therefore, be a diversity of ways to justify human rights philosophically. The different underlying philosophies might well generate disagreement about the proper limits to the exercise of human rights and the correct way to relate different human rights to each other. He warned the world not to expect too much of an International Declaration of Rights. It might be possible to get agreement on words, but agreement on the implementation of human-rights standards would require agreement on values. Given the value diversity of the world, this would be difficult. The best hope was that agreement would be reached on practical rather than theoretical values (Maritain 1949).

Several UNESCO contributors were concerned with the relation between rights and duties. Mahatma Gandhi suggested that all rights had to be deserved by the performance of corresponding duties (Gandhi 1949). E. H. Carr argued that rights implied duties, because governments could not protect the rights of citizens if citizens failed to support their governments and to provide them with the necessary resources (Carr 1949: 21–2). We shall see that, although the relation between rights and duties remains a central problem of human-rights theory, some theorists reject the proposition that the performance of duties is a *precondition* of human rights.

Margaret Macdonald, in an essay written in the late 1940s, at the time at which the Universal Declaration was being drafted, questioned the concept of natural rights from a positivist point of view. How, she asked, could propositions about natural rights be validated? They could not be verified by empirical observation. Natural-rights theorists claimed that these rights were known to 'reason'. Macdonald thought that this appeal to 'reason' was tautological, for to say that human beings had human rights because they were human beings was equivalent to saying that human beings were human beings. Natural-rights theorists might reply that human beings had natural rights because they were rational. Against this Macdonald argued that the supposed fact that human beings were rational did not logically lead to the conclusion that they had natural rights. There was a gap between reason and natural rights that natural-rights theorists had failed to bridge. The appeal of the concept of natural rights, she thought, derived from the emphasis on the individual sufferer from bad social conditions. Nature, however, provided no standards of evaluation. Such standards were the product of human choices. There were many ways to characterize human nature, and philosophers had derived different conclusions from different conceptions of human nature (Macdonald 1963). Macdonald's argument that natural rights are neither empirically verifiable facts nor deductions from self-evidently true premises clarifies the challenge that a justificatory theory of human rights has to meet. Her conclusion that human rights are the products of human choice, however, leaves them with no justification at all. As a response to Nazism, this is not satisfactory.

The United Nations introduced the concept of human rights into international law and politics, therefore, at a time when its philosophical justification was very uncertain. This uncertainty was produced both by the historical critique of the concept of natural rights, which we examined in chapter 2, and by the lack of any philosophical consensus on the basis of human rights at the time at which the Universal Declaration was adopted. Worse, the concept of human rights was called into question by the following arguments, among others.

1   Human rights do not exist in nature: they are human inventions. They are, therefore, neither 'natural' nor 'self-evident', but are morally compelling only if they follow from a morally compelling justificatory argument.

2   Aristotle was right to say that human beings are social animals. A theory of human rights must, therefore, *follow from* and not *precede* a theory of the good society.

3   Since the good of society is prior to the rights of individuals, the duties of individuals to society are prior to the rights of individuals.

4   There are different conceptions of the good society, and there are different conceptions of rights that can be derived from them: there is no universal conception of rights.

5   International human-rights law is the product of political power, pragmatic agreement and a limited moral consensus. It has no deeper theoretical justification. Verbal agreement on general principles may conceal disagreement on the meaning and policy implications of those principles.

The justification of human rights has to confront these arguments. This is the task of human-rights theory.

Human rights theory

Rights

The theory of human rights has many tasks: to explain the meaning of the concept, its justificatory basis, its logic and practical implications, the substance of rights, how rights give rise to obligations, to which obligations they give rise, who has these obligations, and the relation between human rights and other values (Donnelly 1985a: 1).

Human rights must be a special kind of right. They are often contrasted with *legal* rights or *civil* rights that derive from the laws or customs of particular societies. Donnelly says that human rights are the rights one has simply because one is a human being. This is a very common and very unsatisfactory formulation. It is not clear why one has *any* rights simply because one is a human being. It is particularly unclear why one has the rights listed in the Universal Declaration. Indeed, this formulation seems very ill-suited to explain this list. Article 22, for example, says that everyone, '*as a member of society*', has the right to social security. Article 21 says that everyone has the right to take part in the government of his country, but one does not have that right because one is a human being, but because one is an adult citizen: children and foreigners do not usually have this right.

The point of rights discourse, which distinguishes it from other moral discourses, such as those that emphasize duties and/or benevolence, is that, if you have a right to x, and you do not get x, this is not only wrong, but it is a wrong to *you*. The discourse of rights draws our attention to the persons who have *rightful entitlements*. The distinctive value of a right is that it gives the right-holder a special entitlement to press the relevant claims if enjoyment of the right is threatened or denied. This distinguishes having a right from simply enjoying a benefit or being the beneficiary of someone else's obligation (Donnelly 1985a: 1–6, 12–13; 1989: 9–12).

Human rights may not be rights one has simply because one is a human being, but they are rights of exceptional importance, designed to protect morally valid and fundamental human interests, in particular against the abuse of political power. They carry special weight against other claims, and can be violated only for especially strong reasons. Ronald Dworkin has made the influential suggestion that rights are 'trumps', but this is misleading if it is interpreted to mean that rights always defeat other moral and political considerations. Dworkin's view was that rights 'trump' only 'the routine goals of political administration', which is a relatively weak conception of rights (Dworkin 1978: xi, 92). Human rights may be trumps in a stronger sense, in that they override more than routine political policies, but it is not plausible to claim that they override all other considerations. Article 29 of the Universal Declaration provides for the limitation of human rights to meet 'the just requirements of morality, public order and the general welfare in a democratic society'.

Other values

Critics of rights discourse sometimes say that there are more important moral values than rights, and that appeal to rights may undermine these values. Parents, for example, should love their children, and children should respect their parents. If parents or children appealed to their rights, this mutual relation of love and respect would be damaged. However, if parents seriously harm their children, children, or adults acting on their behalf, may appeal to their rights. Rights kick in when other values, which may be ideally superior, fail. People are likely to claim their rights when their enjoyment of the objects of those rights is threatened. Rights are safest, however, if the enjoyment of their objects is normal, and their exercise is rare (Donnelly 1985a: 13–15). A principal justification of rights discourse is that it legitimates challenges to social order when that order is unjust. Where justice prevails, appeals to rights are unnecessary. This answers the objection that the concept of rights undermines social harmony.

Some theorists say that unenforceable rights are not rights at all. One can, however, have a moral right to something even if that right is unenforceable. The Jews in Nazi Germany had many moral rights that were not enforceable. The recognition of moral rights that are unenforceable now may help to get them enforced in the future. Donnelly also makes the point that rights can exist in a hierarchy from local custom up through national and international law to a universalist philosophy. Rights claimants will normally prefer the lowest possible level. It is usually easier and more effective to appeal to a local law than to the Universal Declaration of Human Rights or to the moral philosophy of Immanuel Kant (Donnelly 1985a: 15–21).

Philosophers sometimes talk of 'rights-based' moralities, and human rights may seem to be an example of such a morality. There are good reasons, however, for rejecting this view. Firstly, if rights form the *basis* of morality, it may not be possible to defend rights against their critics by appeal to more fundamental values. Secondly, rights ought to be balanced with other values, and it would be dogmatic to assume that rights are always more fundamental than other values. This allows us to give human rights their appropriate priority. We must nevertheless take account of other values if we are to give a plausible account of the *limits* of rights. The question of whether I have the right to insult another person's religion, for example, cannot reasonably be answered simply by assuming that rights always trump other values, for I should identify and evaluate the moral weight of the other values at issue. Rights are important, but they are not the whole of morality. We can have the right to do something that it is not right to do: to criticize our government unfairly, for example. We can have a moral duty to do something that no one has the right to insist that we do: for example, to give generously to humanitarian organizations. There may be 'a right to do wrong', and there may be a duty of benevolence, to which there are no corresponding rights. Everyone may have the right to certain freedoms, but no one has the right to a free society, since no one can have the obligation to provide a free society. A free society may, therefore, be a collective good that is not reducible to individual rights. There may also be individual and collective justifications for rights. The right to freedom of speech, for example, may be justified by the right of the speaker to express his or her views, the right of the audience to hear those views, or the collective good of a free society. Freedom of the press is more adequately thought of as a collective good of a free society than as reducible to a set of individual rights of publishers, editors, journalists or readers. We do not have a human right to everything that is good, or to everything that we need. We may need to be loved, and it may be good to be loved, but we do not have a human right to be loved, because no one has a *duty* to love us. The relations among rights and other moral values is complex, therefore, even if it is true that human rights are especially important values.

There is a controversy as to who has human-rights *obligations*. The orthodox view is that it is only, or mainly, states that have them. This is doubtful, however. Article 30 of the Universal Declaration envisages human-rights violations by non-state groups or individuals. Concern with powerful non-state actors, such as multinational corporations, and feminist analysis of the 'private' sphere as one in which the rights of women are violated, has led to a new view among human-rights thinkers that traditional human-rights theory has been excessively concerned with the state as the addressee of human-rights claims. It may be countered that the state has the primary obligation to prevent human-rights violations by private corporations and to protect women. There is also a question as to whether, if the concept of human rights is extended to 'private' harms, it would cover a wide range of crimes, and lose its distinctiveness and clarity.

Why should we believe that human rights should trump traditional values that conflict with them? Donnelly argues that the forces of modernization have undermined traditional communities and the protections that they may have given to their members, who now need the protection of human rights, even if the concept is alien to their traditional cultures. There may be merit in political and cultural self-determination, but the concept of human rights sets limits to self-determination for the sake of human dignity (Donnelly 1985a: 82–5). This states the human-rights position well enough, but it does not provide a defence of human rights against those who believe that a culture that violates human rights in certain respects (by privileging a certain religion, for example) is superior to one which adheres more closely to the Universal Declaration.

Donnelly supports his 'modernization' argument with an appeal to the international consensus on human rights, which, he says, is based on 'a plausible and attractive theory of human nature' (Donnelly 1989: 21–4; 1999: 85; 2001: 9). There are *three* bases of human rights here: consensus; a plausible theory of human nature; and an attractive theory of human nature. Donnelly seems to like the argument from consensus, because it avoids controversial philosophical theories of human nature. It is unconvincing, however, not only because it is not clear that a *sincere* consensus exists, but also because consensus is factual not moral, and therefore, in itself, justifies nothing. Donnelly implicitly recognizes this by appealing to a theory of human nature that is 'plausible' and 'attractive', and which is based on the liberal value of autonomy (Donnelly 2001: 11–12). This alternative also raises problems: some cultures do not value autonomy, and even liberals, who do generally value autonomy, disagree about its meaning and importance (Parekh 1994; Kymlicka 1995; Barry 2001).

Human nature

Donnelly rejects the idea that human rights are based on human *needs*, because, he argues, there is no scientific way to establish an agreed set of human needs, and the need for dignity rather than needs as such is the basis of human rights. However, the link between human rights and 'dignity' is as problematic as the link with 'needs': the right to security of person, for example, might be based on human need or a requirement of dignity. Most people most of the time 'need' security, but it is not always needed for a life of dignity: soldiers, for example, can lead lives of dignity without as much security as civilians normally require. The relation between needs and rights is certainly complex. One may need something to which one does not have a right, because it would impose unreasonable demands on others. You have a need for friendship, but you do not have a human right to it, because no one has the obligation to be your friend. Although human rights cannot be derived directly from needs, certain needs, such as the need for food, seem to be the basis of some human rights. A certain level of food may be necessary to a life of dignity, and this may ground the human right to food, but the human need for food seems also to support this right.

The combined use of needs and dignity is implicit in the 'capabilities' theory of Martha Nussbaum. This theory attempts to articulate the basis upon which we recognize others as human beings across historical change and cultural difference. Certain capabilities, according to this theory, are essential to the definition of human beings. These capabilities are derived not from a controversial metaphysical theory of human nature, but from historical evidence. The theory of human capabilities aims to be as universal as possible, crossing religious, cultural and philosophical gulfs, while being sensitive to history and cultural difference. It does not privilege particular interpretations of human nature, but seeks consensus about what is essentially human. Its list of necessary human functions is deliberately vague to allow diverse specifications in accordance with varied local and personal conceptions. The list should, however, be open-ended, because it is the outcome of intercultural exchanges. It consists of human capabilities and limits, for human beings are creatures who are both capable and needy.

What are the implications of this approach? We begin by recognizing that human beings are mortal, and have a general aversion to death, even though they may prefer death to its alternatives in special circumstances. They have bodies. They need at least minimal levels of food, drink and shelter. They begin life as needy and dependent babies. They experience pleasure and pain, and have a general aversion to pain. Most experience sexual desire. They move from one place to another. They perceive the world external to themselves through their senses, they can imagine, think, make distinctions and seek understanding. They have practical reason, think about what makes life good, and seek to act accordingly. They recognize and feel a sense of affiliation with and concern for other human beings. They live in a natural world with which they have to maintain a satisfactory relationship. They play and laugh. They are separate individuals: in all cultures human beings are born and die as individuals, and, however close their relations with other human beings, they relate as separate individuals.

The theory specifies two thresholds. The first is one below which life is not human. The second is one below which life is not good. Insofar as the theory provides for human autonomy, it cannot say too much about how people who have reached the first threshold should proceed to the second. All the basic capabilities are, however, distinct and fundamentally important. There are strict limits to the extent to which it is permissible to trade off an increase in one for the reduction of another. The capabilities may, however, be mutually dependent: we may need to move, for example, to get food.

The validity of the theory of capabilities does not require actual universal agreement. Some objections to the list would confirm some of its components, such as practical reason and the recognition of others. The theory provides for a conception of common humanity, respect for cultural difference, and a basis for criticizing particular cultural practices. The theory is sustained by participatory dialogue among those who interpret its deliberately vague principles differently in response to their different circumstances. The theory, by treating practical reason as a fundamental human capability, respects the value of autonomy. It is therefore consistent with certain basic liberal values. The emphasis on the material conditions of choice is, however, more social-democratic than liberal. The theory is robustly anti-racist and anti-sexist, for racists and sexists deny precisely the conception of common humanity that the theory affirms.

The theory of capabilities is the basis for evaluating traditions, social conditions and societies by reference to the quality of life for each human being in the society. It motivates moral action, Nussbaum claims, because the idea of shared vulnerability underlies the sentiment of compassion and that of human capabilities is the basis of respect (Nussbaum 1992). There are strong similarities between Nussbaum's conception of capabilities and human rights. The capability for practical reason, for example, provides the basis for protecting freedom of conscience. Nussbaum, however, has reservations about human rights. The concept of capabilities, she suggests, is both clearer and has more cross-cultural appeal, although she allows that it may provide the justification for rights claims (Nussbaum 2000: 5, 79, 96–101). There are, nevertheless, two basic objections to the theory of capabilities. The first is that capabilities are natural facts, and thus morally neutral and potentially morally bad: imagination, for example, can be used to create works of art or novel methods of torture. We require a different moral theory to distinguish good from bad capabilities. The second objection is that the theory gives us no guidance when the meeting of one need conflicts with the meeting of another (Gray 1986: 47–9). The answer to the first objection is that the theory identifies the minimal conditions of human flourishing, and this sorts out to some extent good from bad capabilities: art is, for example, more conducive to human flourishing than torture. The answer to the second objection is that basic capabilities have priority over more developed capabilities, and the theory does not make any larger claim to decide priorities. Nussbaum claims neither final authority nor completeness for her theory, but, rather, that it provides a stronger basis for evaluating social policies than its rivals do (Nussbaum 2000). As such, it provides a relatively strong philosophical-anthropological basis for the justification of human rights.

Both the theory of natural rights and the entrenchment of human rights in international law suggest that the content of human rights is relatively fixed. However, conceptions of human rights change over time. Such changes can be explained by reference to changes in values and in threats to those values (Donnelly 1985a: 35). The capabilities theory would distinguish between the more stable and the more dynamic capabilities. It may *explain* changes in rights less well than Donnelly's view that human rights are 'socially constructed' can, but it is better suited to *evaluate* such changes by reference to its conception of the quality of life. Donnelly suggests that human rights create the conditions for healthy development (Donnelly 1985a: 38, 40), but 'social constructivism' cannot explain what healthy development is without relying on a theory such as that of capabilities. Donnelly admits that the constructivist theory requires a 'politically relevant philosophical anthropology' to provide 'a substantive theory of human nature' that would generate philosophically defensible lists of human rights (Donnelly 1985a: 36–7). The justification and objective of human-rights action, he maintains, is to make human beings 'truly human', which brings his theory even closer to the capabilities approach (Donnelly 1989: 17–19, 21).

Conflicts of rights

The concept of human rights has historically been challenged by the philosophy of utilitarianism, as we saw in chapter 2. Utilitarianism rejected natural rights as unscientific and as subversive of social order, and proposed, as an alternative criterion for the legitimacy of governments, the principle of utility, which can be interpreted as the common good, the greatest happiness of the greatest number, the maximization of welfare, or by some similar reading. The concept of human rights was revived after the Second World War as a concept better suited than that of utility to articulate what was wrong with Fascism. The problem with the utilitarian conception of maximizing happiness was that it did not condemn Fascism in principle, and might endorse it in some circumstances. However, even the new concept of human rights recognized the appeal of utilitarianism in Article 29 of the Universal Declaration, which states that human rights may be limited for the purpose, among others, of 'the general welfare in a democratic society'.

We have seen that human-rights theorists often express the relation between human rights and the common good in terms of Dworkin's idea that human rights trump the common good, but the meaning and justification of this formula are typically unclear. If the human rights of one individual should endanger the good of society, why should rights trump the common good? This problem is more difficult if 'the common good' can itself be analysed in terms of human rights. Suppose that, by killing one person, we could use their organs to save the lives of ten? Those ten people have the human right to life, but human-rights supporters would intuitively be reluctant to kill one person to save ten. Doing so could be justified by what is sometimes known as 'the utilitarianism of rights', which says that we should maximize the protection of rights, but human-rights supporters are typically reluctant to sacrifice the human rights of one person to protect those of others. There is no agreement as to how such conflicts of rights should be resolved.

Jones suggests that rule-utilitarianism might paradoxically come to the rescue of human-rights theory here. Rule-utilitarianism says that we ought to live by those rules that best promote the common good. The rule-utilitarian reason for not violating the human rights of one person even to protect the human rights of others is that it would violate a justified rule, and rule-utilitarianism says that this should not be done even if, in the short run, it does more good than harm (Jones 1994: 203–4). This is a plausible solution for those who believe that the human rights of some should never be violated to protect the human rights of a larger number of others, but it is not certain that we should always take this position.

The underlying problem is that human rights are deep values, but, even so, they may conflict with other human rights, or the same human rights of other persons, or with other values. Donnelly's constructivism is useless in the face of such conflicts. The theory of Alan Gewirth offers a solution. Human rights, according to Gewirth, are justified because they are necessary to moral action. When human rights conflict, those rights that are more important to moral action ought to have priority over those that are less important: the right not to starve would, for example, have priority over the right to holidays with pay (Gewirth 1978; 1982). This theory, however, offers no resolution of conflicts between equally important rights.

The concept of 'basic rights' has been adopted by some political theorists, who believe that the concept of universal human rights might be 'imperialistic', and yet who do not wish to abandon the idea of minimal standards of decent governmental behaviour (Walzer 1980; Rawls 1993; Miller, D. 1995). Shue has defined basic rights as those rights, enjoyment of which is essential to the enjoyment of all other rights. To secure basic rights, other rights may be violated, if necessary, but basic rights may not be violated to secure other rights. The concept of basic rights provides some guidance in the face of conflict among rights (Shue 1996). It is not clear, however, that any right is necessary to the enjoyment of other rights. For example, although eating is necessary to the enjoyment of the right to freedom of speech, the *right* to eat is not necessary. Donnelly worries also that the identification of 'basic rights' may lead to the neglect of other human rights, which are, according to his theory, necessary to a life of dignity (Nickel 1987: 102–5; Donnelly 1989: 38–41). The concept of 'basic rights' is, therefore, controversial, and consequently not very helpful in solving the problem of conflict among rights.

Perhaps such conflicts are theoretically irresolvable. If so, this is worth noting, for human-rights discourse is generally reluctant to recognize the possibility of irresolvable dilemmas in moral and political life. This may be because human rights are often expressed as simple solutions to complex problems, and a more complex formulation of rights might resolve some apparent conflicts. The right to freedom of speech, for example, would not conflict with the right not to be subject to racial abuse, if the former were specified to exclude the right to express some forms of abuse (Jones 1994: 199–201).

Steiner argues that conflicts of rights lead to intolerable arbitrariness, and that rights therefore should be 'compossible', that is, only a theory of rights that avoids conflicts is rational. His theory of rights, however, recognizes only rights to private property that exclude most of the economic and social rights recognized by the UN (Steiner 1994). His critics complain that his theory would allow an intolerable trumping of basic human rights by property rights.

There is a common view that only civil and political rights are genuine human rights because they require only inaction by governments (refraining from torture, for example), and therefore can be fulfilled universally, whereas economic and social rights depend on specific, not universal institutions (such as a welfare state), and are too expensive for some governments to afford. There is no duty to do the impossible, and, if it is impossible to respect some economic and social needs, there can be no *right* to have them met (Cranston 1973; Rawls 1999: 80). Shue and Donnelly have answered these arguments effectively. Donnelly points out that the distinction between the two types of rights is confused: the right to property is considered a civil right, for example, whereas it could as reasonably be considered an economic right (Donnelly 1989: 30). Shue argues that failure to respect certain basic economic rights, such as the right to subsistence, would render civil and political rights worthless. Both authors also argue that protecting civil and political rights can be expensive (providing fair trials, for example) and that both types of rights may require positive action or inaction by governments. There is thus no basis for treating only civil and political rights as genuine human rights (Shue 1996; Donnelly 1989).

Democracy

It is commonly believed that human rights and democracy are mutually supportive or related to each other by definition. The Vienna declaration of 1993, for example, asserted that democracy and human rights were 'interdependent and mutually reinforcing'. The relations between the two are, however, quite complex. Similar values, such as respect for the dignity of the individual, may form the basis of both human rights and democracy. Democracy may also be, empirically, the best form of government for protecting human rights, although some electoral democracies fail to protect economic and social rights, while some authoritarian regimes do so quite well (Chun 2001). Nevertheless, human rights and democracy have different, and potentially competing, theoretical foundations. Democratic theory asks who ought to rule, and answers 'the people'. Human-rights theory asks how rulers ought to behave, and answers that they ought to respect the human rights of every individual. Democracy is a collective concept, and democratic governments can violate the human rights of individuals. The concept of human rights is designed to limit the power of governments, and, insofar as it subjects governments to popular control, it has a democratic character. But human rights limit the legitimate power of all governments, including democratic governments. Human rights are consequently often protected by entrenching them in constitutions. This transfers power from democratically elected political decision-makers to judges, who are usually not democratically elected.

Waldron has made a rights-based critique of the constitutional entrenchment of rights. He argues that, if the value of human rights derives from the dignity of individuals, the outcome of democratic participation by such individuals should have priority over the judgements of courts (Waldron 1993). Dahl argues, similarly, that the people are the best judges of what is good for them, and are, therefore, the safest guardians of their rights. Democracy is, in this sense, prior to rights (Dahl 1989). Dworkin, however, makes a distinction between majoritarian and egalitarian democracy. Majoritarian democracy permits the 'tyranny of the majority', and is a defective form of democracy, since it denies the equality of all citizens. Egalitarian democracy recognizes the equality of all citizens, and therefore entrenches their rights in a constitution to protect them from violation by majorities. The constitutional protection of democratic rights is, according to Dworkin, not undemocratic, because it is intended to protect democratic equality (Dworkin 1978; 1996). This dispute is difficult to resolve, partly because it involves complex empirical questions about the outcomes of court decisions. Most actual democracies entrust the protection of basic rights to independent courts. However, neither courts nor elected legislatures guarantee the defence of human rights or democracy. Some theorists argue that a strongly supportive political culture is a better safeguard for human rights and democracy than specific institutions.

Conclusion

The concept of human rights is often criticized because it is 'individualistic', emphasizes rights *rather than* responsibilities, and encourages selfishness. Locke's classical theory of natural rights, however, was based on natural law that imposed an obligation on everyone to respect the rights of others. The concept of rights can be used selfishly, but all concepts can be abused: the concept of duty, for example, can be used by the powerful to control the weak. Rights advocates often fight for the rights of others, and are, in doing that, not acting selfishly. Article 29 of the Universal Declaration of Human Rights assumes that everyone has social duties, and Gewirth argues that the concept of human rights entails duties to communities that sustain human rights (Gewirth 1996). It is sometimes said that the concept of human rights presupposes the concept of the non-social individual. However, the concept of human rights is primarily the basis of a theory of legitimate government. Thus, the concept is so far from being non-social that it is primarily a *political* concept.

The Universal Declaration states that recognition of human rights is the foundation of justice in the world. The relation between human rights and justice has proved to be controversial, however. Liberal theorists of justice have argued that the concept of justice is more fundamental than that of human rights, and theories of justice can say more about how rights should be allocated than the concept of human rights can. The theory of justice can, nevertheless, find an important place for human rights (Barry 1965: 149–51; Beitz 1979). Some theorists believe that whether a human-rights claim is valid or not depends on whether it is endorsed by justice (Cranston 1973: 14). In contrast, Donnelly has argued that the concept of human rights is clearer and less controversial than that of justice (Donnelly 1982). In practice, the concept of human rights may be less controversial than any *particular* theory of international justice, and therefore politically more useful. However, we have seen that many aspects of human rights are very controversial. Liberal theories of justice usually endorse human rights, and it is a matter of practical judgement rather than theory whether a rights-based or justice-based approach to international politics is more effective.

A common objection to the concept of human rights is that rights cannot be derived from nature, but only from the culture and institutions of particular societies. This objection has been made to at least some of the rights in the Universal Declaration. Jones points out that Article 22 says that 'everyone' has the right to social security and to realization, *in accordance with the organization and resources of each state*, of the economic, social and cultural rights indispensable for his dignity. Jones suggests that Article 22 sets out citizens' rights rather than human rights (Jones 1994: 160–3). This should be read, however, as a statement of universal rights that allows the implementation of the rights to vary according to the organization and resources of different states. Insofar as human rights have limits, society sets those limits, and in this sense human rights must be socially and therefore variably specified (Jones 1994: 192–4). Article 29 of the Universal Declaration allows that human rights may be limited by law for certain purposes, though, unfortunately, the wording of this provision is exceptionally vague.

Rights derive from rules governing the relations among human beings. In this sense, rights are essentially social. This is consistent with the idea that rights empower rights-holders. Power is a social relation, and legitimate power is restrained by rules that protect the rights of others. The empowerment of rights-holders is, however, the distinctive feature of rights as a concept. To emphasize human rights rather than human duties is to emphasize the moral worth of the rights-holder without denying that the moral status of human individuals also entails duties to others. The concept of human rights demands respect for human individuals as moral agents and concern for them as vulnerable creatures. It is neither egoistic nor anti-social. It denies neither individual responsibility nor the value of community. It is a concept that affirms human solidarity while respecting individual autonomy. Maritain and Forsythe may be right to say that, given the religious and philosophical diversity of the world, and the 'essentially contested' nature of philosophy itself, consensus on the 'philosophical foundations' of human rights may be impossible to achieve. This is not a serious blow to the concept of human rights, however, because the very idea of philosophical foundations is problematic (Rorty 1993). There are various strong reasons for supporting human rights, derived from respect for human dignity (Donnelly), the bases of moral action (Gewirth), the demands of human sympathy (Rorty), or the conditions of human flourishing (Nussbaum). Human rights do not constitute the whole of morality or politics: they have to be balanced with other values, such as social order. They are not absolute, for human rights can conflict with each other. The moral and humanitarian case for assigning the concept of human rights to a leading role in political theory is, however, very powerful.

5

The Role of the Social Sciences

Introduction: human rights and social science

The origin of the concept of human rights is found in theology, philosophy and law. The concept of natural rights was developed first to articulate Christian theories of wealth and poverty, and then, in the seventeenth century, to defend property and what we now call civil and political rights against absolute, monarchical government. As such it was *normative*: that is, it prescribed how people ought to behave. The contemporary concept of human rights has inherited this normative character: it is designed primarily to prescribe to governments what they ought and ought not to do. Between the French Revolution and the establishment of the United Nations, the natural-law concept of natural rights was challenged by the philosophy of scientific positivism, which strongly influenced the emerging social sciences. According to this philosophy, science is not normative: it does not tell people how they ought to live. That the concept of human rights might cause problems for the social sciences became apparent as early as 1947, when the executive board of the American Anthropological Association submitted a statement on human rights to the UN Commission on Human Rights while it was drafting the Universal Declaration. The statement expressed the concern that a universal declaration of human rights might show insufficient respect to the different cultures of the world (American Anthropological Association 1947). The statement was criticized within the anthropological community on the ground that the association, as a scientific organization, had no business speaking about human rights, for there was no scientific approach to human rights (Steward 1948; Barnett 1948).

The gulf between the normative concept of human rights and the social sciences has been filled largely by law. Law is normative, but it is also factual, as is the degree of compliance with the law: we can study how law is made, interpreted and implemented. There is, therefore, a variety of social behaviours involving human rights that can be studied by the social sciences. The concept of human rights is also political. The normative principles of human rights can motivate people to struggle for the entrenchment of human rights in law. The political sociology of law is therefore an important social science for understanding human-rights social action. The comparative study of social movements may help to explain variations in the making and implementation of human-rights law. The *interpretive* social sciences, such as anthropology and certain approaches to sociology, can also make advances on the dominant legalistic discourse of human rights by explaining how human-rights problems are understood in different cultural settings. The concept can be taken to refer not only to a body of more or less authoritative law, but to a set of *social practices* (including legal practices) that can be studied by the methods of the social sciences. Interpretive social science can bring the concept of human rights down from the heights of philosophy and law to the everyday lives of the ordinary people it claims to defend (Preis 1996).

The dominance of law

Before the 1970s almost all academic work on human rights was done by lawyers, and most articles were published in law journals. A survey of journals published between the early 1970s and the mid-1980s conducted by the UN Economic,

Social and Cultural Organization (UNESCO) found that almost all human-rights journals were predominantly legal, and that the social sciences contributed little to other journals that carried articles on human rights. Several surveys on the teaching of human rights in universities have shown that the legal perspective is overwhelmingly dominant. The legal approach to human rights cannot adequately analyse the ethical, political, sociological, economic and anthropological dimensions of human rights. Human-rights law has social and political origins, and social and political consequences, and legal analysis cannot help us to understand these. The social sciences have substantive interests and research methods that are quite different from those of legal studies, and which can illuminate the social practice of human rights (Pritchard 1989). The social sciences have, however, until recently largely neglected human rights.

Law is concerned primarily with *judgements* as to whether human rights have been violated or respected. The task of social science is to *explain* respect for and violations of human rights. Judgemental disciplines sometimes make assumptions about the measures that will reduce the quantity or severity of human-rights violations. Social scientists test causal hypotheses empirically, and can thereby contribute to effective policy-making (McCamant 1981).

Political science

Political science neglected human rights between the adoption of the Universal Declaration in 1948 and the mid-1970s, except for some descriptive studies (McCamant 1981: 532). This neglect is explained by two main influences on the discipline: realism and positivism. Realism taught that politics was overwhelmingly the pursuit of power, and that ethical considerations, such as human rights, played at most a marginal role. Positivism taught that social scientists should eliminate ethical judgements from their work, because they were unscientific and 'subjective'. This situation began to change in the 1970s, especially during the period of the Carter presidency in the USA, because human rights were becoming part of the reality of international politics.

In 1976 an important pioneering work in the political science of human rights, edited by Richard Claude, appeared. Claude argued that human rights could not be understood by the analysis only of legal processes. Social scientists should investigate the social forces underlying human-rights development. This would involve both historical and comparative approaches. Claude described the 'classical' pattern of human-rights development in France, Britain and the USA. He argued that, in the process of the development of a mature human-rights regime, four problems must be solved: the securing of political freedom; the guarantee of legal rights; the establishment of the right to political participation on the basis of equal citizenship rights; and the recognition and implementation of social and economic rights.

Claude developed several empirical hypotheses from his comparative historical analysis:

1　The more people engaged in private economic activity, the more likely were legal guarantees for freedom of expression.
2　The stronger the demand for citizenship equality, the stronger the state became.
3　The more elites competed for support, the more they would encourage popular participation and civic equality rights.
4　The more poor people participated in politics, the more likely was the implementation of economic and social rights.

The 'classical' model, therefore, proposed an economic basis for the institutionalization of human-rights law in the emergence of private, capitalist economies. The development of a mature human-rights regime involved the sequential introduction of three forms of decision-making: market exchange that required legal security; bargaining that extended rights to new social forces; and central decisions to regulate and administer an increasingly complex set of rights. Human rights developed in these countries in a context of relatively gradual social and economic change, and conclusions drawn from the study of these processes might well not apply to those countries that were undergoing, or at least attempting, rapid change. Claude suggested that this might lead to more centralized decision-making that would prevent the emergence of a human-rights regime according to the classical model (Claude 1976).

In the same volume Strouse and Claude found by statistical analysis that rapid economic development had a negative effect on political rights. They concluded that developing countries often faced painful trade-off dilemmas between the protection of civil and political rights, on the one hand, and rapid economic growth, on the other (Strouse and Claude 1976). This implied that it was impossible for governments to pursue rapid economic growth and protect civil and political rights. Statistical analysis cannot, however, show that this is impossible – only that it is unusual.

Donnelly examined the relation between economic development and human rights with a different method. He identified three supposed trade-offs in this relation. The *needs* trade-off sacrificed basic needs to investment. The *equality* trade-off is based on the belief that great inequality is necessary to rapid economic development. The *liberty* trade-off assumes that political rights encourage populist policies that obstruct economic growth. Trade-off ideology says that human-rights violations will be temporary, for economic development will eventually meet basic needs, reduce inequality and protect civil and political rights. Donnelly tested the empirical truth of this ideology by a comparative study of Brazil and South Korea.

By the 1970s Brazil had grown sufficiently to meet the basic needs of the poor and to reduce inequality. It failed to do this, because the rich were powerful, and used their power to defend existing inequalities. The flaw in trade-off theory is that it assumes that the rich and powerful will in time protect the rights of the poor and vulnerable. Brazil shows that this may not happen. It does not, however, show that human-rights violations are *necessary* for rapid economic growth. South Korea between 1960 and 1980 achieved more rapid economic growth than Brazil with much less inequality and relatively good protection of social and economic rights. It also had special features that statistical analysis might overlook, such as cultural homogeneity, the economic benefits of Japanese colonialism and US aid, and social discipline in the face of the security threat from North Korea. The case of South Korea refutes the hypothesis that the needs and equality trade-offs are *necessary* for rapid economic development. Its record of civil and political human-rights violations during this period was, however, very bad. Political repression often accompanies economic development, but it does not necessarily lead to it. The unanswered question is whether political repression is *necessary* to economic growth. Rapid development creates winners and losers, and the winners may need to repress the losers. However, even if this is true, it does not show that *any* political repression can be justified for the sake of development. The precise relation between political rights and development remains an open question. Donnelly believes that the more developed a country, the less justified repression becomes, and that repression may lead to a crisis of legitimacy, as, for example, in Indonesia. The liberalization and democratization of developed authoritarian societies may, therefore, help to stabilize them (Donnelly 1989: 163–202). Against this, it can be argued that liberalization and democratization may themselves be destabilizing, as the cases of the USSR and Yugoslavia show, especially if they are not accompanied by further economic development. How to stabilize a democratizing regime is currently a central question of political science.

In 1986 Ted Gurr showed how positivism could be used to study problems related to human rights. He bypassed the problem that human rights is a normative concept by studying state violence, which he did by using a basic model of regimes and their challengers. He treated violence as one of many policy options for states seeking to establish and maintain their authority. He then put forward fourteen hypotheses about the state, its challengers, ethnicity and class, and the global environment. Examples of these hypotheses are: the greater the threat posed by challengers, the more likely the state is to use violence; the greater the ethnic diversity and the social inequality, the more likely the state is to use violence; states facing external threats are more likely to use violence internally (Gurr 1986). The empirical testing of these hypotheses should explain variations in the levels of state violence. Some of Gurr's hypotheses are interesting: for example, the hypothesis that states ignored by the international community because they are economically or militarily insignificant are more likely to use violence. However, Gurr leaves the relations among the hypotheses unclear. For example, threats to the state tend to increase state violence, but democratic institutions tend to reduce state violence. What happens if there is a great threat to a democratic state? Gurr suggests, perhaps correctly, that the level of state violence would increase, but he offers no explicit answer to this question. The hypotheses also do not explain the *dynamic* of violence. For example, in the former Yugoslavia, ethnic diversity may have been correlated with state violence, but this explains very little about what happened in that society after the fall of the communist regime.

Whereas Gurr sought to explain state violence by reference to the state and its challengers, Foweraker and Landman ask how popular social movements can establish rights regimes. The social-movement approach is related to Gurr's state-centred theory insofar as social movements struggle to get states to recognize and enforce rights. The relation between social movements and rights is dialectical in that movements seek rights, and rights empower movements. Social movements do not, however, necessarily lead to the establishment of rights. They can be counter-productive, and lead to increased repression. The state may, however, have an interest in buying legitimacy by granting concessions in the form of rights. Historically, economic forces have combined with philosophical theories to demand and legitimate a new legal regime based on the protection of capitalist property rights and the civil and political rights of citizens. The best guarantee of rights is provided by the combination of active non-governmental organizations and an independent, competent and non-corrupt judiciary. The discourse of rights has instrumental value because it creates solidarity among those with similar interests, and it can easily be applied to new struggles over different issues and in different cultural contexts. It can thereby create solidarity among those with different, and even to some extent incompatible, interests, such as women, ethnic minorities and indigenous peoples. Finally, social movements seek to close the gap between law and politics, between 'rights in principle' and 'rights in practice'. However, as societies move from authoritarianism to democracy, the protection of rights may move to the legal sphere, and social movements may lose their pre-eminent role. Foweraker and Landman claim that comparative, empirical, quantitative analysis shows that popular social forces can make democracy and are not condemned to be victims of historical forces beyond their control. Although their own empirical study is limited to four similar cases – Brazil, Chile, Mexico and Spain – they conclude by suggesting that this qualified optimistic message has global implications (Foweraker and Landman 1997).

The study of Foweraker and Landman has limitations. It restricts itself to civil and political rights and excludes economic, social and cultural rights. It studies 'citizenship rights' and ignores 'human rights'. Nevertheless, it shows how comparative, empirical, statistical political sociology can illuminate the relation between social movements and legal rights. It is a strong antidote to excessively legalistic approaches to rights.

Sociology

Political science has shown ambivalence towards the concept of human rights, because it has been influenced by positivism, which is hostile to the concept of rights, and by normative political philosophy, which is the source of the concept. Sociology has had less to say about human rights, because it shares with political science the influence of positivism but has, historically, distanced itself from its origins in political philosophy. However, Foweraker and Landman have shown the social nature of struggles for rights.

The sociologist Bryan Turner has extended this analysis by arguing that the institutionalization of human rights through the United Nations is an important feature of the social process of globalization, and human rights can be viewed, in sociological terms, as a global ideology. Turner draws on Max Weber's argument that the historical 'rationalization' of society had undermined the religious and metaphysical foundations of law and rights. Positivism and relativism were the consequences of secularization. This explains why the UN, in adopting the Universal Declaration, transformed the meta-physical concept of natural rights into the secular concept of human rights. From a sociological point of view, however, human rights are 'social facts' without inherent value. Turner agrees with Foweraker and Landman that the concept of citizenship has been closely linked with the modern nation-state, but argues that this political form has been infected by numerous problems, such as imperialism, globalization, regionalization, migrant workers, refugees and indigenous peoples, which raise questions about the nation-state as the framework for an adequate analysis of citizenship and rights. As globalization has created problems that are not wholly internal to nation-states, so the concept of citizenship rights must be extended to that of human rights. Sociologically, the concept of human rights can be explained by the need to protect vulnerable human beings by social institutions, which in their turn pose threats to those human beings. The social and legal institutionalization of human rights is the pre-dominant modern attempt to resolve this dilemma that is inherent in modern societies (Turner 1993, 1995).

Malcolm Waters argues that a sociological theory of human rights must take a social-constructionist approach that treats the universality of human rights as itself a social construction. On this view, the institutionalization of human rights reflects the prevailing balance of political interests. The rise of rights discourse is not to be explained, as Turner argues, by human vulnerability and institutional threats, but by the assertion of class interests. The original specification, and the subsequent elaboration and enforcement, of the Universal Declaration can be explained by reference to four sets of interests: the interest of the allied victors of the Second World War in stigmatizing and penalizing their defeated enemies; the interest of the cold-war powers in undermining each other's legitimacy; the interest of superpowers in legit-imizing intervention in the affairs of other states; and the interest of disadvantaged groups in claiming rights against the state (Waters 1996). This is an interpretation of some well-known features of modern history in terms of a realist theory of interests. It downplays ideals, and consequently cannot explain the role of human-rights organizations that work for the rights of others.

Stammers criticizes legalistic and statist approaches to human rights on the ground that human-rights violations occur at the sub-state, social level. The power perspective on human rights which he advocates can show that economic and social rights are often violated by private economic agencies, and that the human rights of women are violated by men. Those who, like Donnelly, see states as the solutions to human-rights problems may be mistaken, because they locate human-rights obligations where the power to solve human-rights problems may be lacking. Also, in looking to states to solve human-rights problems, statists may have to advocate an increase in the power of states, which is the original source of human-rights problems. Statist solutions are inherently elitist and discourage democratic solutions to human-rights problems. The institutionalization of human rights may also lead, not to their more secure protection, but to their protection in a form that is less threatening to the existing system of power. The *sociological* point is not that human rights should never be institutionalized, but, rather, that institutionalization is a social process, involving power, and that it should be analysed and not assumed to be beneficial. Similarly, social movements do not necessarily promote human rights, and human rights are not promoted only by social movements, even though social movements can play a role as supplements to institutions in the protection of human rights. The power perspective requires us to consider the impact of institutions and social movements on the distribution of power, and not merely on the legal formalization of rights (Stammers 1999).

Rhoda Howard had earlier argued, in an analysis of human rights in Commonwealth Africa, that a society's capacity to realize human rights was strongly affected by its social structure. The most enduring cause of human-rights violations was social and political inequality. Commonwealth Africa had been affected by three overwhelming economic circumstances: the colonial heritage of raw-material extraction and labour exploitation; its extremely vulnerable position in the world economy; and the domination of its economies by the state and ruling classes. These economies were peripheral to the global capitalist economy and consisted of a mixture of capitalist and pre-capitalist forms. Most of the population were peasants whose income depended either on world market prices or on those paid by state monopoly marketing boards. The state extracted the surplus value of peasant labour in order to fund itself and subsidize the capitalist and urban sectors. The dispersal, low educational levels, and economic hardships of the peasants made it difficult for them to mobilize in social movements for human rights. The state controlled the economy, and consequently state elites were intolerant of oppositional actors, who were potential economic as well as political challengers. This inhibited the rise of bourgeois challengers to the state. Post-colonial rulers had inherited authoritarian forms of governance from their colonial predecessors, including the practice of executive interference with the judiciary. African states were also authoritarian because they were weak: they lacked both the legitimacy and the administrative structures to regulate society, and so resorted to rule by coercion. The legitimacy of the state was weakened by its failure to build nations from the diversity of ethnic groups. The ethnic conflict that was common in Africa could not, however, be explained by ethnicity alone, but had to be understood by reference to state power and social inequality.

Howard's structural approach to the sociology of human rights did not exclude the role of culture. Pre-colonial Africa was generally characterized by communalistic cultures, in which human worth was recognized by reference to social roles and statuses rather than to individual rights. Such values were not so much 'African' as typical of pre-capitalist societies. Africa had, however, interacted with international capitalism for some five centuries, and contemporary African societies were significantly marked by capitalist structures and values. Modernization (especially urbanization) had substantially disrupted traditional social organization, and thereby much of its traditional culture. Social roles and statuses had become more differentiated and fluid. Consequently, many Africans were adopting more individualistic values. They had to deal with the modern African state and dominant class as modern individuals without the support of traditional institutions. African communalism and cultural relativism had become myths that were used by modern elites in their struggle to dominate modern professionals and intellectuals. Traditional African culture was incompatible with human-rights standards in some ways, especially with regard to the status of women and children. However, contemporary Africa was not predominantly traditional, but, rather, a modern society with modern political and economic problems. Human-rights literature, Howard argued, had neglected the constraints on the realization of human rights caused by differential access to material resources and political power. It had been characterized by *legal idealism* devoid of *sociological realism*. Legal reform was insufficient to improve human rights: structural change was necessary (Howard 1986).

Howard left unclear how, if social structure was the main cause of human-rights violations, structural change for human rights was possible. Later, she suggested that liberal capitalist societies produced the structural changes that were necessary for the development of the concept of human rights. These changes produced the concept of the private person and the self-determining individual (Howard 1995). Here Howard meets the limits of sociology that were identified in chapter 2. The structural explanation of human-rights violations and the rise of human-rights ideology can provide no ethical justification of human rights. Howard's sociology shows how social structure may lead to human-rights violations and obstruct change. It may even suggest how change may come about. But it cannot, as she wants it to, tell us why we should welcome such changes. The attempt to move from positivist analysis to ethical advocacy is unsuccessful.

Whereas Howard's sociology of human rights is an uneasy combination of Marxist structural explanation and liberal ethics, Woodiwiss adopts a 'discourse' approach. Whereas the former is based on the study of the relatively unsuccessful economies of Commonwealth Africa, the latter derives from the analysis of the relatively successful economies of East and South-East Asia. Woodiwiss makes use of the concept of 'patriarchalism', which he defines as a discourse that assumes the naturalness of social inequalities and justifies them by reference to the respect due to a benevolent father. The concept of 'enforceable benevolence' refers to a form of governance where the content of benevolence is democratically decided and legally enforced. Woodiwiss maintains that patriarchalism and human rights can be mutually compatible, and that 'enforceable benevolence' may provide the basis of an alternative human-rights regime to those of liberalism and social democracy defended by Donnelly and Howard. He argues that liberal rights would be unenforceable in patriarchalist societies because of their deferential culture. He rejects Howard's suggestion that modernization tends to create a convergence on similar conceptions of human rights. In making this argument, Woodiwiss assumes that the culture of deference is unchangeable, whereas his own analysis shows that it is not. Thus, he fails to dissociate liberalism from human rights in principle: at most he shows that liberal human-rights principles may be difficult to implement in certain cultural contexts.

Over the past hundred years or so, Woodiwiss argues, humankind has been organized into a global entity with an identifiable institutional structure and an emergent ideological dimension in the form of the discourse of human rights. The law in capitalist societies provides an ideological reinforcement of social relations by ordering them in terms of rights and duties. The rule of law is not identified with a particular political philosophy, such as liberalism, but with a social-structural effect: the reduction of arbitrariness. How the law can defend human rights must, therefore, vary with its social-structural context. The effectiveness of a human-rights law may depend, not only on local class relations, but on wider, transnational economic forces.

Woodiwiss argues that what he calls 'American social modernism' (roughly, the Universal Declaration conception of human rights defended by Donnelly) has been the principal ideological support for the discourse of human rights in the Pacific region since 1946, even though some of these rights, especially those relating to labour, are in decline in the USA as a consequence of the arrival of 'postmodern' (so-called post-industrial) society. This has left a space for Japanese capitalist patriarchalism to assume a dominant ideological position in the Pacific region. This patriarchalism, Woodiwiss says, is likely to offer more to workers in the Pacific region than Western conceptions of workers' human rights. The labour law and the human-rights regime that stand the best chance of being respected are those that are constructed in such a way that they mobilize the patri-archalist cultural and social-structural biases in their favour. The case studies show that there is widespread, latent po-litical support for a labour-law system and human-rights regime based on 'enforceable benevolence'. This may become an Asian way in which the Eurocentrism of human-rights discourse may be overcome.

Woodiwiss concludes that there is no fundamental incom-patibility between patriarchalism and human rights, because rights can be expressed in values and institutions that do not endorse autonomy. Human rights, therefore, do not, contrary to the argument of Donnelly, require a liberal-democratic state or individualistic values. Patriarchalism, Woodiwiss ar-gues, is as compatible with respect for human rights as lib-eralism, except in the area of gender relations. The exception of gender relations is, of course, a large one, and the disso-ciation of human rights and liberalism is derived, not from the sociological analysis of Asian patriarchalism, but from a redefinition of the concept of human rights to sever its con-ceptual link with equality.

Capitalism is, Woodiwiss believes, intrinsically subversive of respect for human rights. As a set of structural relations and a source of motivations, capitalism requires that indi-viduals are treated differently depending on how they are positioned within the relation of capital and labour. This positioning determines what freedoms individuals have. By contrast, the discourse of human rights requires that individ-uals are treated in the same way regardless of how they are positioned within any set of social relations. Capitalism's tendency to subvert human rights may, nevertheless, be countered by structural demands for order and/or legitimacy (Woodiwiss 1998). What Woodiwiss shows is that *both* patri-archalism and capitalism are social systems of structured inequality that undermine the liberal ideal of equality em-bodied in the concept of human rights. What he does *not* show is that progress towards greater equality of rights is impossible in the patriarchalist societies of East Asian or in any other capitalist societies. His sociological analysis pro-vides a salutary reminder of structural and cultural barriers to the achievement of equal human rights. It does not *refute* the 'social modernism' of Donnelly, but it does emphasize the *structured* obstacles to human-rights progress in a global capitalist world characterized by cultural diversity.

Psychology

Woodiwiss argued that sociology can provide a more powerful analysis of human-rights realities than psychology can. It may be thought that psychology is not a *social* science at all, since it is a science of the (individual) human mind. However, human-rights behaviour is the product of the human mind, and psychology therefore should contribute to our understanding of it.

A psychological concept that is highly relevant to human rights is sympathy. Most human beings suffer when they know that others are suffering. However, we suffer most when those who are suffering are close or similar to us. We are, for example, much more upset by the suffering of our own children than that of strangers in distant lands. We are, therefore, more likely to act to help our nearest and dearest, and to be indifferent to the suffering of distant strangers. In some cases, we may feel hostile to strangers, and, at the extreme, we may see certain others as not human, and therefore not entitled to the benefits of normal moral restraints, that is, as having no human rights. Sympathy may, therefore, inhibit human-rights violations, while limited sympathy may enable them to occur.

A related concept is that of cruelty. Governments may violate human rights 'rationally', as an efficient means to achieve certain ends. Some violations, however, are not efficient in this way, and exhibit cruelty that is inefficient or even counter-productive. The cruel part of human nature cannot explain human-rights violations by itself, for it is developed, channelled, inhibited or let loose in particular social situations. It is unlikely that we could adequately explain the mass murder of the Jews without reference to the psychology of Adolf Hitler, but it is certain that we cannot explain it only by reference to his psychology, since his murderous desires must themselves be explained, and could be implemented only under certain social conditions.

Another approach to the explanation of some human-rights violations is provided by *scapegoat theory*, which is derived from *frustration-aggression theory*. This latter theory says that a frustrated person tends to become aggressive. The obvious target for this aggression is whoever is responsible for the frustration (the frustrator). There are, however, at least four reasons why the frustrated person may not target the frustrator. Firstly, the frustrated person may not know who the frustrator is: for example, an impoverished peasant in Africa may not know who is responsible for their condition. Secondly, the frustrator may be known but inaccessible: our peasant may know, for example, that the International Monetary Fund (IMF) is responsible for their impoverishment, but have no way to get at the institution. Thirdly, the frustrator may be too powerful: if the army has stolen the peasant's crops, the peasant may not attack the army for fear of reprisal. Fourthly, the frustrator may be protected by the local culture: if the Church is to blame for the frustration, for example, there may be an inhibition that prevents aggressive retaliation. If aggression cannot be directed at the frustrator, frustration-aggression theory says that it is likely to be *displaced* onto another target. Scapegoat theory says that, since aggression cannot be directed at the frustrator because the frustrator is unknown, inaccessible, too powerful and/or morally protected, the probable target of *displaced aggression* is a person or group that is known, accessible, weak and despised. Ethnic minorities often have these characteristics, which is why they are often the target of irrational aggression.

Experimental psychology has shown that ordinary moral individuals are likely to conform to the standards of their group or to the orders of a person in authority, even if doing so violates their own moral values (Glover 1999: 294; Milgram 1974). These experiments suggest that gross human-rights violations are likely to occur when murderous leaders mobilize the co-operation of ordinary followers, who do not question their social environment or their leaders. However, studies of those who rescued Jews during the Holocaust suggest that actions to defend human rights may be motivated, not by rational and independent moral thinking, but by conformity to groups or authority figures that are themselves humane (Hallie 1979; Tec 1986; Oliner and Oliner 1988).

Anthropology

We have seen that anthropology in the USA after the Second World War was dominated by a mixture of positivism and relativism. In the 1960s relativism was picked up by radical anthropologists to challenge the authority of the discipline's elites and their supposedly 'imperialist' approach to other cultures (Washburn 1985, 1987; Spiro 1986). The epistemological requirement that anthropology be scientific was in tension with the ethical requirement that anthropologists ought not to harm, and perhaps ought to defend, the interests of the peoples whom they studied (Washburn 1987).

In these debates human rights played little role. Some anthropologists, however, began to combine the 'committed' anthropology of the radicals with ideas from the growing human-rights movement. Survival International, in the UK, and Cultural Survival, in the USA, were activist organizations that brought together academic anthropology and a concern for the rights of tribal or indigenous peoples. A volume entitled *Human Rights and Anthropology* was published by Cultural Survival in 1988. The editors acknowledged that the peoples whom anthropologists studied were often victims of serious human-rights violations. Anthropologists had expressed concern for human rights through their professional associations, but the discipline of anthropology had neglected human rights. Anthropologists should investigate those state policies directed towards eliminating cultural pluralism. Such investigations were both scientifically justified and ethically required (Downing and Kushner 1988). Downing suggested that anthropology could contribute to the understanding of human rights and cultural diversity by showing how conceptions of rights functioned in different cultures and how cultures incorporated external ideas (Downing 1988). Barnett argued that anthropologists were sensitive to the value of different cultures to those people whose cultures they were, but could also recognize that they might be internally oppressive. The recognition of cultural difference, therefore, did not rule out intervention in other cultures, but it did impose the obligation to respect the context into which that intervention was to be carried out (Barnett 1988). Doughty pointed out that, in Latin America, the concept of 'citizenship' had traditionally been defined so as to exclude indigenous peoples, with the result that these peoples had become victims of gross human-rights violations. Anthropologists had ignored state policies towards cultural difference. This was a scientific and moral error (Doughty 1988). Schirmer emphasized the cultural character of human rights, and argued that the question for anthropologists was not that of the relation between universalism and relativism, but that of the relation between the human-rights culture and other cultures (Schirmer 1988).

Ellen Messer has pointed out that the UN human-rights system is predominantly *legalistic* and *statist*. Anthropologists see law as only one type of cultural system, and so anthropological conceptions of human rights are likely to differ from legal conceptions. Anthropologists should, however, no longer study 'cultures' as local, isolated entities, but as part of an interactive and interdependent global system of cultures. The debate between universalism and relativism can be transcended by recognizing that cultures change and that human rights must be implemented in a world of cultural diversity. Anthropologists can help the cause of human rights by clarifying the relations between international human-rights law and particular cultures. These relations may be conflictual, and the conflicts should be resolved through dialogue and understanding, not by cultural arrogance and coercion (Messer 1993).

Richard Wilson complains that the discourses of legal positivism and socio-political realism favoured by governments and human-rights NGOs misrepresent the subjective experiences of the victims of human-rights violations, and are consequently morally questionable features of a highly moralistic discourse. The abstract universalism of human-rights discourse often ignores local contexts and thereby misunderstands the social and cultural dimensions of conflicts over rights. Human-rights law speaks in a clear and certain voice, while human-rights experience is complex and uncertain. In order to move beyond subjectivity to authoritative objectivity, human-rights discourse paradoxically dehumanizes its subjects. The task of anthropology is to put the human back into human rights (Wilson 1997a; 1997b).

Schirmer and Stoll argue that decontextualized universalism can lead to counter-productive international interventions for human rights, either because of undue emphasis on legal reform with neglect of social consequences, or by oversimplifying what may be complex social and political relations. Anthropology can help to make human-rights interventions more effective by providing them with a deeper understanding of their cultural, social and political contexts (Schirmer 1997; Stoll 1997). Although this anthropological perspective may support a valid critique of some human-rights initiatives, we should remember that international human-rights organizations often employ anthropologists and other country specialists, and so their ignorance of local conditions should not be exaggerated.

International relations

Anthropology, which has traditionally studied local cultures and neglected larger political structures (and therefore human-rights violations perpetrated by states), has now begun to link local cultures with international forces. The academic discipline of international relations also neglected human rights for many years, because it was dominated by the realist theory of states that saw them as motivated by self-interest and not by ethical concerns such as human rights. A partial exception consisted of studies of human rights in US foreign policy, inspired to a large extent by the efforts of President Jimmy Carter to incorporate human rights into his foreign policy in the late 1970s.

R. J. Vincent was a pioneer in introducing the study of human rights into international relations. He held that human rights were marginal to international relations, and states often used the idea to promote their own interests, but, nevertheless, the concept of human rights had become part of global law and morality. After the Helsinki Conference on

Security and Co-operation in Europe in 1975, at which the USSR accepted human rights in principle, human rights became a salient feature of cold-war international relations. In the same period, human rights entered international relations between the rich North and the poor South, with the latter emphasizing economic and social rights and a collectivist conception of rights, especially the rights to self-determination and development, whereas the North tended to give priority to civil and political rights. The concept had been incorporated into international relations in such a way that no state could ignore human-rights considerations in its foreign policy. Nevertheless, foreign-policy professionals were typically wary of human rights, preferring standard-setting to implementation, generalities to specificities, and viewing human rights as one of the *problems* of foreign policy rather than as the solution to problems. Against this view, Vincent argued that the cautious and carefully judged incorporation of human rights into foreign policy might promote the interests of states. Human-rights foreign policy should concentrate on those violations that were the most serious and most open to change. He thought that emphasis on subsistence rights best met these two criteria (Vincent 1986).

The concept of human rights can be incorporated into the academic discipline of international relations through the use of regime theory. We saw, in chapter 3, that the international human-rights system can be considered to be a regulatory regime. Donnelly has classified regimes as declaratory, promotional, implementation, and enforcement regimes, each of which can be classified as relatively weak or strong. The international human-rights regime is a relatively strong promotional regime, a relatively weak implementation regime, and not an enforcement regime. The explanation for the general weakness of the regime is that, while it was relatively easy to establish a declaratory human-rights regime in reaction to Nazi atrocities after the Second World War, because the costs of doing so were small, states have had no interest in developing a stronger regime. A strong human-rights regime would threaten the foreign policies of powerful states and the power of many insecure rulers. The international regime is weak because it is seriously under-resourced by those states that claim to promote human rights, and, in Donnelly's view, because it takes an excessively legalistic approach to human-rights problems whose causes and solutions are political. The explanation of the existence of a weak human-rights regime is that moral concerns are not wholly absent from foreign policy, and there is a weak tendency to consistency, so that one self-interested condemnation of a human-rights violation can lead to another that is not wholly self-interested. International human-rights regimes can help states that wish to improve their human-rights performance by political support and technical assistance. The European regime is relatively strong because the moral commitment of European states is relatively strong and the risks to states' interests are small. The inter-American regime has been quite active, despite, or because of, the gross human-rights violations in its region. Donnelly attributes this activity to the dominant role of the USA. Africa has a very weak regime, and Asia and the Middle East have no regimes, because moral commitment to human rights among elites is weak and state interest in not having such a regime is strong (Donnelly 1989: 206–18, 252–8).

There has been a considerable growth in human-rights regimes since 1945, both of general rights and of more specific rights, such as those of workers and women, and against racial discrimination and torture. This growth has been largely in declaratory and promotional regimes. The move to implementation and enforcement regimes poses greater threats to state sovereignty, and has therefore been extremely slow and uneven. Human-rights regimes show that moral concerns play some part in international relations, although this is marginal. These regimes are strongest among states for whom they are least needed, although they may effect marginal improvements in these states, and are least likely to develop among states in which human-rights violations are very bad. Generally, human-rights regimes *reflect* states' commitment to human rights; only marginally do they *strengthen* that commitment (Donnelly 1989: 223, 227–8).

Human rights may enter international relations multi-laterally – through regimes, for example – or bilaterally, through the foreign policies of states. Donnelly identifies three sets of ideas that inhibit the inclusion of human rights in foreign policy: realism, statism and relativism. Realism says that states are self-interested and do not pursue moral goals.

Statism says that states ought not to interfere in each other's internal affairs. Relativism says that they ought not to impose their values on others. Donnelly concedes that there may be some merit in each of these principles, but none excludes human rights from foreign policy, for the self-interest of states may include the promotion of human rights; the principle of non-interference is qualified by the obligation to protect human rights; and there is some cross-cultural consensus for human rights. States have a range of means to influence human rights in other societies, from 'quiet diplomacy' through economic sanctions to military intervention. All suffer from two defects: the states using these means will usually be motivated to a large extent by self-interest, and the 'target' state may have a strong interest in resisting the pressure. This does not mean that foreign policy cannot improve human rights – only that its achievements are likely to be limited and uneven.

Powerful states are generally unwilling to intervene for human rights, unless the moral case is very strong and the likely costs very low. Even if such an intervention does take place, and succeeds in preventing serious human-rights violations, the task of reconstructing a stable, rights-respecting society through external military force may be formidable. The controversial military intervention by NATO in Yugoslavia to protect the human rights of ethnic Albanians in Kosovo is a good example. Donnelly concludes that the protection of human rights is primarily a national rather than an international problem (Donnelly 1989: 229–37, 242–9; 1998: 85; 1999: 90–1). The case for caution about military intervention for human rights is strong, but the argument that peoples must emancipate themselves, though appealingly democratic, may leave many peoples oppressed for a very long time.

Donnelly argues that, because the concept of human rights was promoted by the United Nations and incorporated into international law, the importance of the international level of human-rights protection has been over-emphasized, and the contribution that the discipline of comparative political science might make to our understanding of variations in respect for human rights in different societies has been seriously underestimated (Donnelly 1989: 260–9). This argument has merit, but requires two qualifications. The first is that the academic discipline of political science has, by its positivistic insistence on being 'scientific' and value-free, neglected the value-laden subject of human rights. The second is that the *interaction* between international and national forces hostile to, and supportive of, human rights is likely to be more important, empirically, for understanding national human-rights performance, and consequently more important for the policy of promoting respect for human rights.

The boldest attempt to integrate the national and international levels of human-rights analysis has been made by the 'boomerang theory' of Thomas Risse and his colleagues (Risse, Ropp and Sikkink 1999). This theory argues that human-rights improvements in repressive states are most likely if pressure by social movements within nation-states is supplemented by other states and non-governmental organizations, and then 'boomerangs' back onto the target state, thereby creating more freedom for national pressure groups. The success of the 'boomerang' strategy is by no means guaranteed, but it offers the best hope for human-rights reform. We shall examine this theory in more detail in chapter 7.

Both the legalistic and the liberal, political-science approach to human rights have been criticized on the ground that they emphasize states too much and neglect the role of private economic organizations, especially multinational corporations, in the violation of human rights, in particular economic and social rights. The emphasis of human-rights discourse on the relations between individuals and governments neglects, it is said, the *structural* causes of human-rights violations. Human-rights activists and scholars have been reluctant to talk about *capitalism* (Evans 1998). The discipline that would investigate the structural, economic causes of human-rights violations is *international political economy* (IPE). IPE may be the most neglected discipline in the field of human-rights studies. However, although it has much to contribute, it has its dangers, since it may under-emphasize precisely the well-being of *individuals* that lies at the heart of human rights and the *subjective* experience of human-rights violations underlined by anthropology. IPE is similar to the discourse-sociology of Woodiwiss, and has similar merits and limitations: it emphasizes the structural causes of human-rights violations but under-emphasizes the potentialities of human-rights activism.

Conclusion

Nietzsche called ethical idealists 'emigrants from reality' (Glover 1999: 29). The task of the social science of human rights is to bring human-rights supporters back to reality. This reality is one both of objective processes and structures and of subjective meanings and values. A social science of human rights demands both sympathy and scientific rigour. The concept of human rights lies in a domain in which normative philosophy, law and social science meet. Social science is not enough, for it cannot guide our lives. Philosophy may offer to do so, but it is a weak motivator to action. Philosophy and social science should clarify our understanding of human rights, but neither is necessary or sufficient for doing the right thing. Understanding human rights requires us to understand both the contribution and the limits of philosophy and science. Social science is itself a social process, and its connection with human rights is problematic. Science has been historically connected with the idea of emancipation from authority and ignorance, and therefore with freedom and well-being. But the scientific philosophy of positivism can lead down the path of moral indifference, while the 'interpretive' social sciences, such as anthropology, can lead to moral relativism (Bellah et al. 1983: 1–6).

Albert Hirschman has argued that the modern social sciences have been characterized by an 'anti-moralist petulance' that can be traced back to Machiavelli's anti-moralistic political science. Social scientists have a 'trained incapacity' to take morality seriously. Somehow the analytical rigour of science and ethical seriousness have to be brought together (Hirschman 1983: 21–4, 30). Robert Bellah maintains that the division that we make between social science and philosophy arises from an attempt to 'purify' these disciplines. There may be advantages in this differentiation, but the division between science and ethics has costs that can be met only by intellectual activity that crosses the boundaries we have set up. Positivism in social science sought to reject ethics in order to improve the quality of knowledge that it produced. Ironically, it failed, because it failed to understand itself as a social practice that was inescapably ethical. Like all social practices, social science takes place in a field of power. If it fails to recognize this social fact, it is more likely to serve the powers that be. A social science of human rights must have other purposes, and thus must be self-conscious about its ethical commitments (Bellah 1983).

6

Universality, Diversity and Difference: Culture and Human Rights

The problem of cultural imperialism

The Universal Declaration of Human Rights states, in Article 1, that all human beings are born equal in rights. The Vienna Declaration of 1993 affirms that all human rights are universal, indivisible and interdependent. Human-rights theorists commonly say that all human beings have human rights simply because they are human beings (Gewirth 1982: 1; Donnelly 1985a: 1; 1999: 79).

We have seen that these claims that human rights are universal are not literally supported by the text of the Universal Declaration. Article 25, for example, says that motherhood and childhood are entitled to special care and assistance. According to the declaration, some human rights belong only to special categories of human beings. The Vienna Declaration recognizes a number of special categories, such as women, children, minorities, indigenous people, disabled persons, refugees, migrant workers, the extremely poor and the socially excluded. We need to understand how there can be special categories of human-rights holders if everyone is equal in rights 'without distinction of any kind', as the Universal Declaration proclaims.

Some human rights are simply universal: the right not to be enslaved, for example. Other human rights are universal only *potentially*. There are two kinds of these rights. The first consists of rights that are activated only in certain unusual situations: the right to a fair trial, for instance. The second consists of rights that are activated when human beings meet some criterion – becoming an adult, for example – that most human beings meet. The other special categories mentioned in international texts, such as women and minorities, do not have special human rights, but are thought to be especially vulnerable to human-rights violations.

According to some critics of human rights the claim that human rights are universal ignores the fact that human beings are different. Universality, they say, is an illusion produced by the dominance of Western states over human-rights discourse since the Second World War. The 'universality' of human rights is an ideological disguise for 'cultural imperialism'. The tension between universality and difference in the concept of human rights was expressed in the Vienna Declaration, which affirmed the universality of human rights, but qualified this affirmation by insisting that 'the significance of national and regional particularities and various historical, cultural and religious backgrounds must be borne in mind.'

In the run-up to the Vienna conference, there had been much discussion of a challenge to the idea of universal human rights from certain Asian states and intellectuals. There was said to be a distinctively Asian conception of human rights. The basis for this challenge was said to be the different cultures of non-Western societies and/or the special needs of poor countries (Tang 1995). Although some human-rights supporters believe that these appeals to difference are ideological disguises for oppressive practices of authoritarian governments (Christie 1995), some universalists believe that universalism has to take cultural diversity seriously (Donnelly 1989: part III; Baehr 1999: chapter 2). A broader and deeper challenge to human-rights universalism maintains that it belongs to 'the Enlightenment project' of philosophical ratio-nalism and to an outdated 'social modernism' (Woodiwiss 1998) associated with nineteenth-century ideas of science-based progress and mid-twentieth-century ideals of social democracy. These ideas have been challenged by a politics of 'difference' based on a 'postmodern' philosophical 'decon-struction' of universalist certainties. The first wave of challenges to imperialism, based on liberal and democratic human-rights principles, has been superseded by a second wave, based on the anti-universalist celebration of cultural difference. As a result, simple human-rights universalism has to compete with alternative cultural perspectives and the view that there are different cultural interpretations of human rights (Chan 1999; Othman 1999).

It is commonly said that the concept of human rights is based on a Western conception of liberal individualism, and that this conception has no roots in many non-Western cultures (Aidoo 1993; Bell et al. 1995). Some scholars are very sceptical of the claim, commonly made in UN circles, that the concept of human rights has roots in non-Western cultures (UNESCO 1949: 260; Chun 2001: 21). Donnelly argues that problems now discussed in terms of human rights were traditionally treated in non-Western cultures, as in the pre-modern West, in terms of 'the right' and of duties, but not of human rights. In these cultures, there might be rights derived from the community and its different status-positions, but not *human* rights (Donnelly 1985a: 49–51, 86). There is merit in Donnelly's argument, but it is overstated. Islamic scholars who derive human rights from our obligations to God are employing an argument similar to Locke's. Islam may be reluctant to recognize that Muslims and non-Muslims are equal in rights, but Locke was reluctant to recognize equality between Protestants, on the one hand, and Roman Catholics, atheists and heathens, on the other. Donnelly might say that the modern concept of human rights is more egalitarian than Locke's, but, if Western natural-rights theory could evolve into the modern concept of human rights, Islam may be able to evolve in a similar way. Donnelly is correct to distinguish the concept of human rights from different concepts such as justice and obligation, but, in his treatment of non-Western cultures, he underestimates the capacity for various moral concepts to develop into human-rights conceptions.

There is no doubt that there are cultures which are, in important respects, incompatible with human rights. This is, however, not a new problem. Classical natural-law theory was familiar with cultures that supported practices that it condemned (Tuck 1979: 85). Natural law did not simply entail the *imposition* of Western values on non-Westerners, because it might entail *obligations* of Westerners to respect the rights of non-Westerners, as in the natural-rights theory of Locke. Universalism can recognize diversity in two ways: (1) by insisting that some moral rules apply in all cultures, despite their diversity; (2) by explaining how universal principles may require diverse interpretations and applications in different social contexts: the right to a fair trial, for example, does not require identical trial procedures in all countries.

It is ironic that human-rights universalism should be accused of 'cultural imperialism', since its origins lay in opposition to Nazi imperialism. Almost no critics of universalism and defenders of cultural difference oppose the *universalist* condemnation of racism that is one of the most fundamental human-rights principles. However, some principles of the Universal Declaration have more cross-cultural appeal than others. Article 16, for example, sets forth a liberal right to marry. Saudi Arabia objected to this at the time of its drafting on the ground that it was objectionable to Islam (Morsink 1999a: 24). While anti-universalists rely on universal principles (the value of cultural difference, for example), even Western liberal philosophers can be sceptical about strong universalist moral claims (Rawls 1999).

International human-rights institutions have generally accepted that universal human-rights standards ought to be interpreted differently in different cultural contexts. The International Covenant on Civil and Political Rights, for example, provides that, in the election of members of the Human Rights Committee, consideration be given to the representation of different forms of civilization and different legal systems. The committee itself has said that the right to family life may vary according to socio-economic conditions and cultural traditions (Robertson and Merrills 1996: 64). The European Court of Human Rights has employed the concept of 'margin of appreciation' to recognize national differences in the interpretation of European human-rights standards (Arai 1998; Gross and Aoláin 2001). Universal standards are modified legally by the reservations that states make in ratifying human-rights treaties. Since the question of universalism *versus* relativism in human rights is usually represented as a cultural contest between the West and the Rest, it is worth noting that the USA has been particularly unwill-ing to accept international human-rights standards (Forsythe 1995: 301). While there is a mixture of consensus and reser-vation about human rights at the legal level, there has been much disagreement at the political level, especially about the relation between human rights and international economic justice. This has usually taken the form of arguments about the priority of, on the one hand, civil and political rights, and, on the other hand, economic, social and cultural rights. The Universal Declaration, implicitly, and the Vienna Declaration, explicitly, affirmed the 'indivisibility' of these two kinds of rights, but the two covenants of 1966 and much actual prac-tice treat them differently.

Donnelly allows that collectivist cultures with no concep-tion of human rights may be morally defensible in conditions of extreme scarcity, when social solidarity is necessary for sur-vival. He argues, however, that the capitalist economy and the nation-state have in most places separated the individual from the small, supportive traditional community to a signif-icant extent. Appeals to cultural tradition in these circum-stances are often made by authoritarian elites who have little or no regard for the traditional cultures of their societies. Modernized elites often invent pseudo-traditional customs to defend their repressive and corrupt regimes from criticism. Many gross violations of universal human-rights standards are the products of distinctively modern forms of rule, and have no basis in traditional culture. In such conditions the individual needs human rights for the protection of human dignity, and thus the concept of human rights has 'near universal contemporary relevance' (Donnelly 1989: 59–60, 64–5). This argument, too, has merit, but it may also be too sweeping. The actual relations between modernization and traditional cultures may be quite complex, and the human-rights package that actually emerges, and the one that would best protect the dignity of all concerned, may have to be based not only on abstract universal principles but also on a sensitive reading of local traditions.

If the concept of human rights is valid at all, extreme relativism is invalid, since it would entail the rejection of universalism. Human-rights universalism, however, entails some diversity of human-rights practice, since the concept of human rights presupposes the value of autonomy, which would lead to some variation in human-rights practice in different cultural and socio-economic conditions. The most difficult case is that in which those who are victims of human-rights violations support the culture that legitimates those violations. Women who are malnourished or uneducated, for example, sometimes support the cultures that place them in this condition. Nussbaum argues that the expressed opinions of the victims cannot be morally decisive, because the very injustice that denies them food and education denies them the ability to imagine alternative ways of life and therefore to express alternative desires. Their apparent satisfaction with their condition, far from justifying it, is part of what is wrong with it (Nussbaum 1993). The apparent consent of those who lack the resources for dissent is a false consent, and justice requires that the weak have the real capacity for choice. Cultural relativism is biased against the weak. Cultures may therefore be interrogated at the bar of justice (O'Neill 1993). It is common in these situations to call for 'dialogue', but this may be an inadequate solution if the victims of an unjust culture are unable to participate in the dialogue. Forceful intervention from outside may have undesirable consequences. There is no general solution to this problem, but we can say that it would involve both the kind of cultural critique proposed by Nussbaum and O'Neill, and a contextually sensitive understanding of the likely consequences of different types of intervention. Although Donnelly concedes that there may be some rare circumstances in which universal human rights might justifiably be overridden by an incompatible local culture, he generally holds a fairly strong form of human-rights universalism, to be enforced by states. This perhaps underestimates the extent to which some people find dignity in conformity to their culture just because it is *their* culture, and may find rights-enforcement by even a liberal state as an unwelcome intervention in their way of life (Donnelly 1989: 110–16).

Even strong universalists usually allow considerable variation in the form in which human rights are implemented, for example in legal procedures. Since human-rights principles are very general, they must be interpreted in order to be applied, and interpretation is a cultural process. In the absence of an authoritative global interpreter of human rights, this interpretive process must vary somewhat in different cultural contexts. This raises the problem that the difference between 'interpreting' human rights in a culturally specific way and undermining their universal applicability may be difficult to determine. Getting the balance between universality and cultural difference right is helped by clear reasons for the universal principle and for the local interpretation.

The critique of human-rights universalism on the ground that it is based on Western liberalism has been accompanied by a Western critique of liberalism by the so-called communitarian philosophy that finds liberalism, and therefore, by implication, the concept of human rights, too 'individualistic' and insufficiently concerned with the common good of human communities (Waldron 1987: 151, 166–209; Mulhall and Swift 1996). This is a complex debate (Caney 1992), but the charge that the concept of human rights entails the neglect of community is unfounded. Since Locke, theorists of rights have emphasized the necessity of community for the protection of rights (Gewirth 1996). Communitarians sometimes say that the 'individual' who is central to liberal, human-rights theory is too 'abstract', but the 'community' that is central to communitarian theory is equally abstract. In particular, communitarians often neglect the extent to which communities are structured by power; how power is used to oppress some members of the community; and the extent to which even small communities can be characterized by internal disputes about community values. The concept of human rights recognizes that communities consist of vulnerable individuals, while not denying that communities may be necessary to the flourishing of individuals. Communitarianism may tend to support cultural relativism against human-rights universalism, but many communities have incorporated some conceptions of human rights into their cultures in order to combat oppression by states or larger communities within which they live.

We have seen that human-rights universalism is sometimes accused of 'cultural imperialism'. The concept of human rights is, however, universal and *egalitarian*: all human beings are equal in rights. Imperialism is by its nature *inegalitarian*, and objections to imperialism normally assume some form of moral egalitarianism. Thus, the concept of human rights, far from being imperialistic, provides the basis for criticizing imperialism. Those who criticize human rights for being imperialistic assume that anti-imperialism is itself a universally valid principle, but typically do not make clear to which universal principles they are appealing in condemning imperialism. In the classical Lockean theory of natural rights, imperialism is immoral because it violates the right to political self-determination that is itself derived from the natural right to freedom. There is, therefore, a strong, rights-based liberal argument against imperialism. Some argue that this rights-based liberalism is itself culturally Western, and that to universalize it is imperialistic. The merit of liberal universalism, however, is that it offers freedom and rights to everyone equally. The defect of the anti-imperialist critique of liberal universalism is that it appears incoherently to oppose the universalization of freedom in the name of a universal right to freedom. It is a common fallacy that cultural relativism supports anti-imperialism, but it does not, for cultural relativism provides no basis for criticizing imperialistic cultures. If anti-imperialism is universally valid, it must be based on some universal principles. The liberal principles of human rights are strong candidates for being the best available anti-imperialistic principles.

Cultural relativism

The anti-imperialist argument against human-rights universalism may be popular because it is thought to express two ideas that have widespread appeal: (1) everyone is equally entitled to respect; (2) to respect a person entails respect for that person's culture, because culture constitutes, at least in part, a person's identity. However, these principles are inconsistent with cultural relativism, because they are universal principles. Cultural relativists find it difficult to avoid the temptation of deriving relativism from universal principles, which explains why cultural relativism appears to be attractive, but in fact does not make sense. The principle that we should respect *all* cultures is self-contradictory, because some cultures do not respect all cultures. The principle of respect for persons does not entail that we ought to respect all cultures, and therefore cultures that endorse the violation of human rights cannot demand our respect simply because they are cultures. Cultures that are incompatible with universal human rights in some respects may have some value, but cultural relativism fails to provide a general objection to human-rights universalism. It is inconsistent to support human rights and respect cultures that violate human rights. Human-rights supporters should, therefore, realize that they are committed to not respecting some cultures, or at least some features of some cultures.

The argument against human-rights universalism on the basis of cultural relativism is often confused with arguments based on state sovereignty, because both are used to keep outsiders from interfering with the internal affairs of a society. The logics of these two arguments are, however, quite different, and, to some extent, mutually incompatible. The appeal to state sovereignty is not an appeal to cultural relativism, because the principle of state sovereignty is as universal as that of human rights. The principle of state sovereignty may have some value in discouraging unwarranted interference and in keeping the peace among states, but it may also protect human-rights violators, and it may help states to crush cultures. It is important, therefore, to distinguish arguments about sovereignty from arguments about culture.

Culture may properly enter into the implementation of human rights in a different way. Human-rights principles are abstract and general, but must always be implemented in complex, particular situations. These situations will always include local cultures. If the justification of human rights is the protection and promotion of human dignity, the implementation of human rights must take into account local cultures and the contribution that they may make to human dignity. The implementation of human rights, therefore, cannot be derived directly from international texts, but must be mediated by judgements about particular local circumstances, including local cultures. We must remember, however, that even local cultures may be contested by those people whose cultures they undoubtedly are. Too often, a mistaken respect for culture involves taking the interpretations of dominant elites or majorities as representing cultures at the expense of subordinate groups or minorities.

Cultural relativism may appeal to some because the 'philosophical foundations' of human rights are supposed to be problematic. The philosophical foundations of human rights are problematic, however, because the philosophical foundations of all beliefs are problematic. It follows that the philosophical foundations of cultural relativism are also problematic. In this situation, it may be helpful to ask whose interests are served by human rights and by cultural relativism. Human rights are designed to protect the fundamental interests of everyone. Cultural relativism may protect vulnerable cultures from 'imperialistic' invasion, but we have seen that it can also protect oppressive elites. Well-intentioned Western liberals, even human-rights supporters, sometimes succumb to the appeal of cultural relativism from fear of appearing imperialistic or even 'racist'. Sensitivity to the dangers of cultural arrogance is proper, but collaboration with oppressive cultures is not.

If we are to respect the cultures of other peoples, we must know what those cultures are. It is often difficult for outsiders to acquire this knowledge in a reliable form. Governments and intellectual elites often act as 'gatekeepers', offering an official version of the people's culture to the outside world. We have, however, theoretical and empirical grounds for being sceptical of the claims of elites to speak for the people. The voice of the people is the expression of its culture, and we can hear the voice of the people only if the people have a secure set of rights. If some people are, for example, not free from the fear of arbitrary arrest, or if women are excluded from public life, we cannot know whether the culture of the people is being truly represented. Respect for cultural diversity, therefore, which is often represented as a threat to the universality of human rights, may, quite to the contrary, require the robust implementation of those rights.

Donnelly holds that human rights are universal partly because the conditions that produced them in the West – capitalism and the nation-state – have become globalized. This process of globalization has, however, consisted not simply of the spread of Western culture, but also of *domination* by the West and the denigration of non-Western cultures. Many non-Western peoples wish to adopt much of Western culture, especially technology and certain forms of social organization, such as the nation-state and some form of capitalist economy, but the colonial experience has often produced ambivalent attitudes to the West. Cultural assertiveness may, in these circumstances, be an expression of dignity (Taylor 1997). This may appear as the defence of conservative against liberal values, but, in historical context, it can also be a claim for equality against domination. Resistance by some non-Westerners to the concept of human rights, or their insistence on developing their own conception of human rights, may be part of this self-emancipation from Western domination. The concept of human rights may, as David Hitchcock has said, appear to 'come out of the West', as the 'black ships' of imperialism once did, bringing overbearing demands to formerly subjugated and humiliated peoples (Hitchcock 1994: xii), and the concept of universality appears to be a thin disguise for Western cultural, and perhaps political and economic, domination. Insofar as these attitudes are barriers to the implementation of human rights, they must be taken into account. They do not invalidate the concept of human rights, but they do indicate that the concept of 'implementing' human rights is more complex than it is sometimes assumed to be.

In relating human-rights universalism to particular cultures, human-rights scholars generally start with universal human-rights standards, and then judge the various cultures of the world by those standards. This seems reasonable, as the Universal Declaration proclaims itself to be 'a common standard of achievement' for all peoples. However, from the perspective of non-Westerners, this may appear as Western cultural arrogance. They may accept the force of human-rights principles, but see the task of relating them to established cultures not as one of *judging* those cultures, but of *incorporating* human-rights standards into those cultures.

Norani Othman has argued that human rights should be implemented on the basis of a recognition of local cultural distinctiveness. In Western societies, the increasing influence of human rights has accompanied the secularization of public life. In Islamic societies, secularization has not been as thorough-going, so that religion and modernity remain in a state of tension. In this situation, some Muslims have sought an interpretation of human rights grounded in the *Qur'an*. The basis of this interpretation would be the *Qur'anic* conception of universal human nature and ethical universalism. Muslims also believe, however, that change is part of the human condition, so that fundamental Islamic principles have to be interpreted in the light of changing social circumstances.

The acceptance of the UN Convention on the Elimination of All Forms of Discrimination Against Women (CEDAW), Othman says, has been difficult in Islamic societies. Conservatives can represent it as outside interference that is an affront to the autonomy of the society, and mobilize opposition to it on nationalist, cultural or religious grounds. These positions have to be opposed by counter-arguments from within the culture. Human-rights violations have to be shown to be incompatible with the principles of Islam. This is the most effective strategy for improving human rights in Islamic societies and for reconciling universal standards and local cultures. National self-esteem is intimately related to the core national culture, and so human-rights reform must respect that culture. International human-rights standards, and the moral principles on which they are based, which have been derived from Western cultures, cannot be accepted by Muslims until this internal dialogue has taken place (Othman 1999). This proposal has the merit, even from the 'Western', liberal-democratic point of view, that human-rights progress is a matter of self-emancipation and not of external imposition. It leaves unsolved, however, the problem of what external human-rights advocates should do if internal dialogue fails to lead to human-rights improvements.

According to the *Qur'an*, Othman maintains, Muslims are obliged to resist oppression. Thus Islam implies a conception of the person as the bearer of human rights. However, there is a gap in this argument between the *obligations* of *Muslims* and the *rights* of *all human beings*. To reconcile Islam and human rights, Islam would have to recognize the equal worth of Muslims and non-Muslims. Human-rights universalists recognize moral equality among those of different religions. Othman does not show whether this is possible within an Islamic discourse on human rights. This has theoretical significance for the relation between Islam and human rights, and practical implications for those societies, such as Malaysia, in which many citizens are not Muslims.

Othman's argument is primarily *strategic* and *motivational*, although she implies that self-emancipation is superior to external emancipation *in principle*. She argues that the strategy of internal cultural dialogue is preferable because appeals to external standards may be counter-productive. This strategy raises problems of participation by those who do not belong to the dominant culture. It also assumes that the culture in question is isolated from external cultural influences, so that international standards are not themselves already part of the national culture.

Abdullahi An-Na'im has shown that Othman's project could face difficulties. Article 5 of the Universal Declaration says that no one shall be subjected to cruel, inhuman or degrading punishment. Islamic law (*Shari'a*) provides that theft is punishable by the amputation of the right hand. Many people would regard this as violating Article 5. However, *Shari'a* is based on the *Qur'an*, which Muslims believe to be the word of God, and which human beings may not question. They also believe that the punishments decreed by *Shari'a* are rational and humane, because this life is but a prelude to the eternal life, and those who live by *Shari'a* will escape punishment in the afterlife. An-Na'im believes that neither internal Islamic reinterpretation nor cross-cultural dialogue is likely to lead to the total abolition of this punishment in Islamic societies. There are, however, resources in the *Qur'an* for restricting its application, by requiring strict standards of proof, for example, or recognizing various extenuating circumstances (An-Na'im 1992: 33–6). The problem here is that the universal standard is vague, and the Islamic law clear and deeply grounded. We cannot know whether cross-cultural dialogue and/or social changes in Islamic societies will eliminate this punishment. Cautious optimism might be derived from the thought that beliefs about the will of God and appropriate punishment have changed over time in the West, and that there may be some in Islamic societies who support international standards in this matter (Bielefeldt 2000: 107).

Discussion of human-rights universalism versus cultural relativism often contrasts international standards with national cultures. This debate is influenced by the official international system of nation-states. Richard Falk has argued that international human-rights law has been very slow to recognize the values and needs of individuals and groups that are not adequately represented in that system, such as ethnic minorities, indigenous peoples, women, children, gays and the poor (Falk 1992: 48). James Tully has argued that we are now in the third stage of anti-authoritarian politics: the first was the struggle for democratic citizenship; the second the struggle against global imperialism; and the third 'the politics of cultural recognition' (Tully 1995: 15–16). The idea of social exclusion and that of cultural recognition are often confused, but we have to analyse them carefully because, whereas minorities and indigenous peoples may, in some sense, have common cultures, women, children, gays and the poor do not. We have, therefore, to distinguish different types of social exclusion in relation to human rights.

Minority rights

It is often assumed that minority rights belong to the field of human rights (Morsink 1999b: 1053–60), but the relations between the two kinds of rights are complex and problematic. The United Nations, in drafting the Universal Declaration of Human Rights, deliberately decided to leave out minority rights. The League of Nations had had a minority-rights regime, but this was thought to have failed, and the concept of minority rights was believed to have been exploited by Nazi Germany as an excuse for aggression. The Universal Declaration is based on the assumption that individual human rights, including the prohibition of discrimination and the right to practise one's culture, are sufficient to protect cultural minorities. The UN did recognize that there might be a special problem of minorities in setting up its Sub-Commission on Prevention of Discrimination and Protection of Minorities.

The most important provision of international law relating to minorities is Article 27 of the International Covenant on Civil and Political Rights, which provides that, in those states in which ethnic, religious or linguistic minorities exist, 'persons belonging to such minorities shall not be denied the right, in community with other members of their group, to enjoy their own culture, to profess and practise their own religion, or to use their own language.' This goes beyond the Universal Declaration, but contains several problems: (1) it applies only to those states in which minorities exist, thereby encouraging states to deny that minorities exist in their jurisdictions; (2) it recognizes the rights of persons belonging to minorities, not of minorities as such; (3) it imposes on states only duties of non-interference with the rights of such persons, but no duties to assist them.

The reluctance of states to take minority rights seriously has been attributed to the following factors: (1) it would encourage outside interference; (2) minority problems are diverse and it is doubtful that there are universal solutions; (3) minority rights threaten the cohesion of states; (4) rights for minorities would discriminate against majorities (Eide 1992: 221). Nevertheless, the UN adopted, in 1992, a Declaration on the Rights of Persons Belonging to National or Ethnic, Religious and Linguistic Minorities. The title of this declaration follows Article 27 in assigning rights to *persons*, not to *minority groups*. However, Article 1 of the declaration provides that states 'shall protect the existence and the national or ethnic, cultural, religious and linguistic identity of minorities within their respective territories, and shall encourage conditions for the promotion of that identity.' Thus, although the declaration does not recognize minority-group rights, it goes further than Article 27 in imposing on states the obligation to take positive measures to protect minority identities.

The political theory of liberal democracy was not designed historically to solve problems of cultural minorities. The classical conception of democracy entailed the rule of a culturally unified people. In the influential theory of the eighteenth-century French philosopher Rousseau, any cultural differences that might exist in society should be subordinated to the 'general will' of the people (Rousseau [1762] 1968). Locke's liberal theory was designed to protect the natural rights of individuals through government and the rule of law. Locke assumed that, since all citizens were equal, political decisions should be taken by the majority. In this theory, minorities were simply citizens who had been out-voted. There was no conception of cultural minorities. Government had a duty to respect the natural rights of every individual, but minorities as such had no rights (Locke [1689] 1970). Democracy, therefore, emphasized the sovereignty of 'the people', which took priority over minority interests. Liberalism sought to liberate individuals from traditional communities, and therefore gave individual rights priority over group rights. Liberal democracy offers to members of cultural minorities individual rights, including the right to participate in the life of cultural groups. Since it offers these rights to members of cultural minorities on terms of equality with all other citizens, it considers the status of these minorities within liberal-democratic societies to be, in theory, perfectly just. Actual liberal democracies may, of course, be unjust in various ways, but, liberal democrats argue, this is because liberal-democratic principles are often violated in practice. The solution to this problem is the robust implementation of the principles, not their revision.

The persistence of minority claims in even the most developed liberal-democratic societies, the connection between minority problems and gross human-rights violations around the world, and the end of the cold war ideological conflict have generated practical and theoretical challenges to this liberal-democratic solution. In response, a number of liberal-democratic theorists have reviewed the relations between politics and culture, and between majorities and minorities. The concept of 'multiculturalism' has come to occupy a central place in liberal-democratic theory (Gutman 1994). Liberal-democratic theorists are far from agreement, however, on how liberal democracies should solve the problems of multiculturalism.

Will Kymlicka has sought to develop a liberal theory of culture. In a multicultural society, he argues, the state necessarily promotes certain cultures and thereby disadvantages others. In a multilingual society, for example, not all languages can be official languages. This raises the question of justice for minorities. Liberals value individual choice, but individuals make their choices in particular cultural contexts. Liberals should accordingly protect the cultures that provide the bases for individuals' choices. Under certain conditions, cultures can be protected only by recognizing group rights (Kymlicka 1995).

Cultural communities are, therefore, necessary to good individual lives, but individuals ought to have some autonomy from the communities of which they are members to choose the life that seems best for them. Communities are structured by inequalities of power, and are thus always at least potentially oppressive. Liberals cannot, therefore, approve, except under extreme circumstances, the restriction by minority groups of the basic rights of their members. Liberals believe that individuals should have the capacity and freedom to question the culture of their community, and decide for themselves which aspects of that culture they will retain. Some restrictions of individual rights may nevertheless be justified to prevent actions that would undermine communities which are necessary for autonomous choices. What makes this justification of community restriction of individual rights liberal is that its purpose is to protect a rights-supporting community (Kymlicka 1989; 1990; 1995).

Kymlicka does not consider minority rights to be part of human rights, because human-rights principles cannot solve some of the most important problems raised by minorities. Even in liberal-democratic societies, members of cultural minorities may suffer from unfair disadvantages, resulting from the power of majorities, without the violation of human rights. The problem with the concept of human rights is not that it gives the wrong answer to such questions. It is, rather, that it often gives no answer at all. The right to freedom of speech, for example, does not tell us what language policy a society ought to have. The principles of human rights leave such matters to majoritarian decision-making, and this may result in minorities being vulnerable to injustice at the hands of majorities (Kymlicka 1995: 4–5, 109). Human rights may even make injustice worse. For example, the rights to freedom of movement and vote may enable members of the majority to move to the traditional homelands of minorities, outvote them, and then undermine their culture. To protect themselves from this form of oppression, minorities may need collective rights to land ownership and language use, and to restrict the rights to freedom of movement and vote of the majority. Such collective rights are not fundamentally inconsistent with human rights, for liberal-democratic states claim the right to regulate immigration, land use and language policies, and such claims are not usually considered to be human-rights violations. Insofar as the collective rights of minorities resemble recognized collective rights of nation-states, they should be subject to the same human-rights conditions (Kymlicka 2001).

Kymlicka has been criticized for being a liberal imperialist, because he supports minority rights only for minorities that are liberal (Chaplin 1993). Kymlicka might reply that liberals are logically committed to disapproving of illiberal groups. His criticisms of human rights are, however, not compelling. The charge that human-rights principles cannot solve all minority problems can be admitted, for the concept of human rights is intended to set *minimum standards* and not to solve all social problems. The charge that human rights might permit unjust behaviour can be answered by reaffirming that human rights are not unlimited. They may be limited for the sake of protecting human rights or for other reasons, as Article 29 of the Universal Declaration provides.

James Tully has put forward an apparently anti-liberal argument about cultural diversity and justice. He argues that cultural diversity is a fundamental feature of the human condition, and that culture is inherent in human interaction. As citizens interact with each other, so they express their different cultures. Cultural recognition is a basic human need. A uniform political and legal system, to which all citizens are subject in the same way, denies this cultural diversity unjustly. Most liberal constitutions are unjust in this way. Constitutions should consist of a continuing intercultural dialogue. In this dialogue, each speaker should be given their due. This appears to recognize that cultural diversity goes down to the level of the individual, and therefore lays the basis for a conception of (individual) human rights: Tully's 'intercultural' constitutionalism is not as anti-liberal as it appears at first sight. Nevertheless, liberal constitutions, he argues, require cultural minorities to speak in the discourse of the dominant group. They suppress cultural differences and impose a dominant culture, while representing themselves as impartial. By contrast, intercultural dialogue aims for just cultural recognition, while repudiating unjust claims to recognition (Tully 1995). Tully does not make clear his criteria for the justice of claims to recognition, and thereby fails to answer the question to which liberal democracy provides an answer in the form of equal rights for all. Although Tully's theory of intercultural constitutionalism has a liberal core, its reliance on dialogue favours the powerful over the weak, and is therefore in this respect less just than the liberal constitutionalism that he criticizes.

Brian Barry defends a liberal-democratic conception of justice that is 'blind' to cultural difference. Liberalism, he says, accommodates all differences that are just. Liberal democracies are just in that they treat all citizens as equals. They do not tolerate all differences, since some social practices are unacceptably harmful to others and to society. In particular, liberal democracies should not tolerate those who would undermine them. Such toleration betrays justice. In contrast with Tully, Barry opposes the institutionalization of cultural differences, because he believes that this makes minorities more vulnerable to the dominant groups in society. Participation in common institutions creates solidarity, which is the best protection for minorities. Barry's defence of liberal democracy is open to the objection that liberal states cannot be culturally neutral, and that supposedly impartial justice conceals the unjust domination of particular cultures. Barry holds, however, that liberal democracy ought to permit voluntary associations to engage in certain illiberal practices (for example, a religious community can refuse to have women priests) provided that their members have a genuine right to leave (Barry 2001).

In apparent contrast with Tully's emphasis on intercultural dialogue, Barry supports forceful intervention by the liberal state to end unacceptable illiberal practices (for example, the abuse of children) in minority communities. Few people, he argues, object to state intervention in *families* to prevent the abuse of children. Kymlicka is cautious about intervention for two reasons. The first is the unsuccessful historical record of liberal states in their attempts to 'improve' minority cultures. The second is that liberal state agents may be insensitive to the value of minority-group cultures to their members (Kymlicka 1989). We may also recall the argument that self-emancipation is better than emancipation by outsiders. These arguments against intervention are not decisive where the group oppression of its members is extreme.

In liberal democracies, Barry maintains, citizens have no obligation to respect each other's cultures, but, rather, they have obligations to respect each other as citizens, irrespective of culture. This misses Tully's point that citizens encounter each other culturally, and they cannot respect each other as citizens if they despise their fellow citizens' cultures. Barry agrees that cultural differences are unavoidable, but maintains that liberal democracy provides the fairest way of settling disputes among cultures. What all people have in common provides the basis for universal human rights, and their cultural disagreements are best settled by liberal-democratic procedures. Minority rights tend to undermine both human rights and liberal democracy.

While theorists of collective cultural rights sometimes are insufficiently clear that their argument depends on liberal-democratic principles, Barry's defence of liberal democracy underestimates the problem that historical inequalities among cultures pose for liberal-democratic citizenship. If the underlying rationale of human rights is the protection of human dignity, we must be very cautious not to overgeneralize about the institutional requirements of liberal-democratic societies. This is a strong reason for being sceptical about there being *universal* minority rights.

The term 'minority rights' refers to two different kinds of rights: individual rights of minority-group members (for example, the right to vote) and the collective rights of minority groups (for example, the right to education in their native language). The first may be *required* by human-rights principles, whereas the second may be incompatible with human rights (the right to community education may, for example, discriminate against girls). Collective rights can also raise the problem of defining the group that has the rights. If indigenous peoples have rights, for example, who defines who is an indigenous people? Some say that indigenous people should define themselves, but this assumes that (a) we already know who indigenous people are, and (b) there will be no unreasonable self-definition. A further problem of collective rights is that, although it is sometimes assumed that individuals are selfish and groups are not, group rights-claims can be selfish and unjust.

Donnelly argues that, although there are collective rights, there are no collective human rights. Collective rights may be necessary to protect human dignity, and therefore may be compatible with human rights, but, in the event of conflict between collective rights and human rights, the latter should generally prevail. The preservation of cultural groups may be valuable, but, if the group is violating human rights, and its members choose to leave or to abandon its culture, human-rights principles cannot defend the survival of the group. However, since human rights are not absolute, and since rights-violating groups may have some value for their members, there is no general principle governing the right of cultural groups to survival. We should remember, however, that respecting human rights is often the best way of protecting cultural minorities (Donnelly 1989: 149–57). A controversial question is whether cultural minorities have the right to state funding for their culture. It may be good policy for the state to support some minority cultural activities, but it is doubtful whether there is a human right to such support. One problem of recognizing such a right would, again, be that of identifying the right-holders. Critics of such supposed group rights to state support for minority cultures believe that it would encourage competition and division among minority groups and make them more vulnerable to hostility and exploitation by the dominant group.

Indigenous peoples

Minority rights are often confused with the rights of indigenous peoples. Some indigenous peoples' representatives, however, claim that they are not 'minorities', but *colonized peoples*. The confusion is made worse by the fact that there is no agreed definition of either minorities or indigenous peoples in international law or social science. The term 'indigenous people' originates from the American continent, where it refers to those who are descended from the peoples who inhabited the continent before the arrival of Europeans, who, typically, retain a non-European culture, and who are economically, socially and politically oppressed. The application of the concept to other parts of the world is problematic, since some groups who have the social characteristics of indigenous peoples are not indigenous, and some indigenous peoples do not have these characteristics (Kingsbury 1999). Most, though not all, indigenous groups are relatively small, but, together, they constitute between 5 and 10 per cent of the world's population. Historically, they have been victims of genocide, cultural oppression and labour exploitation. Indigenous peoples do not, however, all have similar cultures, nor do they all have similar social problems.

There have been two significant developments in conceptions of the rights of indigenous peoples in recent years. The first has been a move from emphasis on *integration* and *assimilation* to debates about *self-determination*. The second has been a move from the International Labour Organization (ILO) to the Human Rights Commission. Issues concerning indigenous peoples arose in the UN first as questions about the exploitation of indigenous labour. They were taken up by the ILO, and this led in 1957 to ILO Convention 107. This convention was based on the premise that the problems of indigenous peoples could be solved by extending to them the citizenship rights of the dominant population. It did not recognize their specific cultures. Consequently, it was rejected by indigenous peoples. In 1989 it was amended as ILO Convention 169, but this failed to meet their demands and was adopted without their participation. Indigenous peoples rejected these statist, 'top-down' solutions, and began to mobilize with the demand for self-determination as colonized peoples. National governments and the 'international community' have been very reluctant to meet this demand, however. This reluctance has been justified by the so-called saltwater principle, which restricts the right to self-determination to colonized peoples who had saltwater between them and their imperial rulers. Thus, Nigerians had the right to self-determination, but the Inuit of Canada did not. The UN Working Group on Indigenous Peoples, consisting of independent experts, has, with the participation of indigenous representatives, drawn up a Draft Declaration on the Rights of Indigenous Peoples that includes the right to self-determination, but governments have proved unwilling to incorporate this into international law.

The indigenous demand for political self-determination is not usually a demand for an independent state, but for self-government within the state in which they live. Equally important for many groups is the demand for *economic* self-determination. Indigenous peoples are not necessarily opposed to economic development, but they wish to control the form that it takes. This often brings them into conflict with states and private corporations that have other plans for these resources.

Indigenous peoples' representatives also claim the right to *cultural* self-determination. This raises the problem of potential conflict between indigenous cultures and human rights. The UN Human Rights Committee, in considering cases of such conflicts, has sought to strike a balance between the rights of individuals and the preservation of indigenous cultures. These decisions show that the international-law conception of human rights is far from being extremely individualistic. Kymlicka maintains that indigenous peoples are more willing to accept adverse judgements of international bodies than they are of institutions of their own states (Kymlicka 1995: 169). Conflicts between collective indigenous peoples' rights and international, individual human rights may, therefore, not be as intractable in practice as they may appear in theory. It should be noted, however, that the states that have agreed to adjudication by the Human Rights Committee are those with relatively good human-rights records. The international human-rights system may offer least protection to those indigenous peoples who need it most.

The right to self-determination

Both the international human-rights covenants of 1966 state that all peoples have the right to self-determination, but who has this right is controversial. The orthodox view in international law is that it is a right to be free from European imperial rule, and not to be subject to racist domination or alien occupation (Cassese 1995). This view is strongly influenced by particular political phenomena such as the world-wide anti-colonial movement, the campaign against apartheid in South Africa, and opposition to Israeli occupation of Palestinian lands. The right has not been extended to other peoples subject to alien rule, such as the Tibetans. The right to self-determination has been interpreted in international politics for the sake of the stability of the states system. The policy of the 'international community' in this has not been very successful, since conflicts over self-determination have constituted perhaps the most disorderly feature of the states system in recent years (Shehadi 1993). The international community has given priority to the principle of *territorial integrity* over that of self-determination. This has left minority peoples vulnerable to majority oppression, encouraged secessionist conflicts, provoked state violence and gross human-rights violations, and threatened destabilization of the inter-state order.

Political theorists have put forward various theories of self-determination on the basis of liberal-democratic principles. The most influential is the *remedial theory*. This says that states which respect the human rights of their citizens have a right to their loyalty, and there is therefore no right of secession from such states. There is a right of secession only if there are serious and persistent human-rights violations and no solution other than secession is available (Birch 1984). This theory is *liberal* rather than *nationalist*, for the violation of individual human rights rather than national interests justifies secession, although the theory might support national self-determination if the victims of human-rights violations constituted a nation.

Beran has put forward an alternative liberal theory that may be called the *voluntarist theory*. This is based on the liberal value of *individual* self-determination. This entails the right to freedom of association. Any individual who wishes to leave a political community has, therefore, the right to do so. If the majority in part of a state's territory wish to secede, they have the right to do so. Human-rights violations are not necessary to this right of secession. Nor is it necessary that the secessionists are a nation (Beran 1984; 1988). The right to secession is subject to two important conditions: (1) secessionists must respect the human rights of everyone living in the new state; (2) they must also recognize the right to secession of the majority of any territory within its borders. This generates what is sometimes called the 'Russian doll' problem. If all territorial majorities have the right to secede, the states system might split up into ever smaller states, with consequent anarchy. Beran puts forward four answers to this objection: (1) the risk of war may override the right to secession; (2) war apart, the right to secession overrides concerns about the number of states; (3) excessive secession would be checked by the self-interest of potential secessionists; (4) excessive secession can be checked by enlightened concessions by states to potential secessionists. Whether Beran's theory would work in practice is hard to say, since it is rejected by the international community. Theoretically, Beran has difficulty in deriving a *collective* right to self-determination from his *individualist* premises. He says that those with property rights have the right to alter the sovereignty over their property, but, lacking a theory of property rights, this argument is very weak.

The collective right to self-determination may be derived from *democratic* premises. According to democratic theory, the legitimacy of government derives from the will of the people. The self-determination of nations is, therefore, equivalent to democracy. Whatever the arguments for democracy, for those who are democrats, democracy is a *collective* concept, and democratic theory is better suited than liberal individualism to justify a collective right to self-determination.

A collective right to national self-determination can also be derived from *communitarian* premises. Communitarians reject Beran's assumption that national membership is voluntary. Most people are born into their nation; it forms part of their identity (Tamir 1993) and constitutes an ethical community (Miller, D. 1995). Communitarians argue that, if there is a right to national self-determination, it must be a collective right (Raz 1986: 207–9). Margalit and Raz argue that individuals flourish through culture; culture is maintained by groups; the prosperity of cultural groups is therefore necessary to the well-being of their members; and self-determination is necessary for the protection of groups.

Human-rights violations are not necessary to justify the right to national self-determination. The right of groups to self-determination is the weaker, however, the more likely it is that recognizing it would lead to the violation of the rights either of group members or of outsiders (Margalit and Raz 1990). The communitarian right to self-determination is therefore subject to liberal conditions.

Some communitarians provide arguments for the value of *communities*, but not specifically of *national* communities. David Miller argues that *nations* are ethical communities and that states are the most effective co-ordinating mechanisms for nations. Nation-states are therefore the best available institutions for social justice, and this provides the justification for national self-determination (Miller, D. 1995). This theory raises several problems. There are problems, for example, in defining nations, and in showing that they are 'ethical communities'. However, even if these problems could be solved, the theory treats justice and human rights in a questionable way, for it claims only that nation-states are the best institutions to provide justice *for their citizens*. This nationalist theory of self-determination allows at best only weak obligations on the part of nation-states towards the human rights of foreigners.

Practical discussions of self-determination are more concerned with international order than with human rights. Shehadi argues that, in order to achieve its goal of international order, the international community must balance the principle of the territorial integrity of states with the aspirations of aggrieved nations, and that there should be international institutions with the authority to settle self-determination disputes in accordance with the rule of law rather than the rule of force (Shehadi 1993). This proposal tries to combine idealism with pragmatism, but may fall between the two: it may be too idealistic to be acceptable to powerful states and too pragmatic to satisfy the requirements of justice. This shows the great difficulty of reconciling the self-determination of peoples with a world of states.

There is a consensus among practical scholars that the right to *secession* should rarely be recognized, but that states should recognize forms of self-determination that fall short of secession (Hannum 1990; Eide 1993). Many governments, however, fear that self-determination may be the first step to secession. Such fears are often exaggerated, but we cannot say that they always are (McGarry and O'Leary 1993). Self-determination problems can be extremely difficult, but their solutions are likely to require not the abolition of the nation-state, but new thinking about the forms that it might take. Some have maintained that the right to self-determination is *the most important* human right or the *precondition* of all other human rights. Some persecuted nations undoubtedly have strong claims to self-determination. However, we have seen that the idea of a universal human right to the self-determination of peoples raises complex analytical problems and carries great dangers to human rights.

The rights of women

The Vienna Declaration emphasized the human rights of particular groups, such as children, disabled persons, refugees and migrant workers. These are very important, but require specialized treatment, which is beyond the scope of this book. It is necessary, however, to say something here about the rights of women, not only because of the importance of the subject, but also because of the *feminist* challenge to traditional human-rights thinking.

Certain limited forms of the mistreatment of women were the objects of international standard-setting by intergovernmental conferences and the International Labour Organization before the Second World War. In 1945 feminists succeeded in having the equal rights of men and women written into the United Nations Charter and in establishing the Commission on the Status of Women (CSW). The prohibition of discrimination against women was included in the Universal Declaration of Human Rights. The CSW, though hampered by underfunding and the opposition of culturally conservative states, was responsible for the Convention on the Elimination of All Forms of Discrimination Against Women (CEDAW), adopted in 1979. Many states have ratified CEDAW, but it is weakened by numerous reservations. The committee charged with implementing CEDAW is also under-resourced and relatively inaccessible to NGOs (Reanda 1992; Jacobson 1992).

Growing dissatisfaction among women's groups and members of the commission about the slow pace of progress led to the Decade for Women 1975–85, which included three world conferences, held in Mexico City, Copenhagen and Nairobi. The declarations and programmes of action adopted by these conferences were endorsed by the UN General Assembly. The issues thus officially recognized included political participation, education, employment, health, nutrition, agricultural production and marketing, access to credit, housing, industrial development, and the special vulnerability of refugees, the disabled, the elderly and many others. The Women's Decade led to a shift of emphasis from activities specifically related to women to 'mainstreaming', that is, incorporating women's issues in all UN planning. It was also recognized that the situation of women would not be improved unless women were empowered through participation in decision-making. Whether this change of strategy has led to much improvement in the everyday lives of women is uncertain (Reanda 1992).

Feminists have challenged dominant interpretations of human rights, arguing that they are biased against women, because they address violations by states, and ignore the violations that women suffer at the hands of men in the private sphere (Byrnes 1992: 519). In classical natural-rights theory, natural rights are held by all human beings and entail obligations by all human beings. This theory has been translated into international human-rights law, in which the rights are held by individual human beings, but the obligations not to violate those rights are borne mainly by *states*. This element of the dominant conception of human rights is sometimes justified as necessary to distinguish human-rights violations from ordinary crimes (Donnelly 1998: 1; 1999: 85–6).

The Universal Declaration, however, is not so statist, and imposes obligations on states, groups and persons. Article 2(e) of CEDAW imposes on states the obligation to eliminate discrimination against women 'by any person, organization or enterprise'. The Vienna Declaration acknowledged that 'gender-based violence and all forms of sexual harassment and exploitation' were human-rights violations, and Article

4(c) of the Declaration on the Elimination of Violence Against Women requires states to exercise due diligence to prevent and punish acts of violence against women, 'whether those acts are perpetrated by the State or by private persons.' Feminists sometimes cite Article 16 (3) of the Universal Declaration, which says that the family is 'the natural and fundamental group unity of society' and is 'entitled to protection by society and the state' in order to show that the declaration endorses the male-dominated family. Article 16 (3) does not have to be interpreted in this way, however, and there are other provisions of human-rights law that can provide the basis for feminist campaigns. Liberals can reply to the feminist criticism that, by insisting on a protected private sphere, they protect the violation of women's rights by men, with the argument that liberalism imposes on the state the duty to protect everyone from violation of their rights in the private as well as the public sphere.

Feminists argue that the subjection of women in the household often leads to their disempowerment in the public sphere. The distinction between the public domain of the state and the private domain of the family is fallacious, they say, because the family is, in all societies, regulated by the state and its law. Reproduction and child-rearing, usually considered to be private activities *par excellence*, are typically regulated by men to form male and female identities so as to ensure the subordination of women. Some recognized human-rights violations, such as torture, are experienced by women in a distinctive way, for example by sexual violence and/or humiliation. Women suffer much more than men from justifications of the violations of almost all their human rights by appeals to culture. In addition, their access to legal redress is often barred by discriminatory, male-dominated legal systems (Binion 1995; Peterson and Parisi 1998; Ashworth 1999; Desai 1999; Coomaraswamy 1999). Some feminists criticize the concept of equality in human-rights discourse on the ground that it fails to recognize the difference of women's experience. It is valid to emphasize the difference of women's experiences, but the critique of equality for the sake of difference may be counter-productive because cultural groups often justify treating women unequally on the ground of cultural difference.

Feminism has energized the cause of women's human rights, and drawn the attention of the UN, governments and human-rights NGOs to the many serious human-rights violations that are suffered exclusively or predominantly by women. This cause was advanced at the fourth World Conference on Women, held in Beijing in 1995, despite opposition from various conservative groups, religious institutions and states. This has certainly been one of the most significant shifts in the interpretation of human rights in international politics since the end of the cold war. Against the feminist critique of international human-rights law, Fellmeth has pointed out that there are about two dozen significant international legal texts aimed at protecting women's rights. The bias against women is much less in international law than in the difficulty of implementing it (Fellmeth 2000: 727–8).

7

Idealism, Realism and Repression: the Politics of Human Rights

The real politics of human rights

The concept of human rights belongs to the *idealist* tradition in the study of international relations insofar as it sets high ethical standards for governments. The dominant tradition, however, has been that of *realism*, which assumes that the principal actors in international relations are *states*; that states are motivated primarily by self-interest; and that self-interest excludes, or at best marginalizes, concern for human rights. Realism can explain the neglect of human rights by states, but it can explain neither the introduction nor the increasing influence of human rights in international relations.

We saw, in chapter 5, that the concept of human rights can be understood in terms of *regime theory*. International regimes consist of rules and institutions to which states commit themselves. International human rights constitute such a regime, though implementation of the regime is relatively weak. The existence and limited achievements of the regime support the idealist approach to international relations, whereas its limitations and failures can be explained by realism. The international human-rights regime, and its regional versions, especially the European, not only implement human rights to some extent themselves, but also provide the basis for human-rights actions by both governments and NGOs. The international policies of states are dominated by realist concerns, whereas NGOs are more idealistic, but carry less 'clout' in international relations.

The principle and practice of state sovereignty are, therefore, strong barriers to the implementation of international human-rights standards. Another strong barrier is the cultural diversity of the world, and the fact that many cultures legitimate practices that violate human-rights norms. The international human-rights regime is commonly presented as the 'imperialist' imposition of Western values on non-Western societies, but the USA has been reluctant to recognize economic, social and cultural rights and to ratify UN human-rights treaties (Forsythe 1995: 301). State sovereignty and cultural difference provide two strong defences against outside pressures for human-rights improvement, and yet the legitimacy of human rights is sufficiently strong that pressures from governments and NGOs can lead to improvements in the human-rights performance of governments, and even to changes of government that result in dramatic improvements. The desire of governments to benefit economically and politically from 'good standing' in the international community may play a considerable role in this process, but realists would be wrong to insist that the moral appeal of human rights has no effect in international relations (Donnelly 1986: 638, 640; Forsythe 1995: 306).

The remarkable growth of international human-rights law since 1945 and the dominance of lawyers in human-rights institutions and academic human-rights study conceal the priority of politics over law in the struggle for human rights. International human-rights law is made by a political process. Political campaigns play an important role in human-rights implementation. Powerful non-governmental economic organizations, such as multinational corporations, are now recognized as important players in the violation and, potentially, in the promotion of human rights, and *political* pressure on these organizations, especially by NGOs, has recently increased. Lawyers and human-rights activists typically assign a central role to legal processes – such as those of the International Criminal Tribunal for the Former Yugoslavia – in the protection of human rights, whereas political scientists are more likely to consider them to be marginal. Forsythe points out that the dramatic improvements at the end of the twentieth century in Latin America, in the former communist societies of Central and Eastern Europe, and in South Africa owed little to legal processes and much to politics. The dominant human-rights problem in the contemporary world is the gap between human-rights ideals and law, on the one hand, and the reality of gross human-rights violations, on the other. The causes of this gap are not primarily legal or cultural, but political and economic (Forsythe 2000).

The human-rights component of foreign policy is, Forsythe maintains, a central feature of international human-rights politics. States set up international human-rights institutions, support and/or resist their efforts to implement human rights, and are the principal targets of those efforts. NGOs have become increasingly important in international human-rights politics, but their importance derives largely from the influence that they have on the human-rights policies of states. These policies may be influenced by public opinion, and not only in democratic societies. States are often criticized, especially by human-rights activists, for being 'inconsistent' about human rights, but this inconsistency may be the result not only of changing perceptions of the national interest in a changing world, but of the selective attention of public opinion to international human-rights issues (Baehr 1999: 101; Forsythe 2000).

International human-rights politics may seem relatively ineffective if its achievements are contrasted with human-rights ideals, but these achievements may seem more impressive if we remember that there was almost no such politics before the Second World War. After the end of the cold war, the centre of international action for human rights shifted somewhat from the more legalistic UN institutions to the highly politicized Security Council. The so-called second generation of UN peacekeeping operations has combined politics, human rights and military force. Some of these operations have been very controversial, sometimes for using too little force (Bosnia), at other times for using too much (Yugoslavia/Kosovo). Human-rights enforcement by the Security Council may be relatively legitimate and effective, but, because this body is highly political, agreement on action is likely to be rare and selective. This is due not, as is often said, to the 'weakness' of the UN, but to the real political divisions in the world. Military enforcement of human rights

is costly in lives and cash, and may be limited by the unwill-
ingness of public opinion to make such sacrifices. It is also
not necessarily well suited to solving the political problems
underlying the human-rights violations.

Even if governments include the promotion of human
rights in their foreign policies, this will be only one among
several elements, and will usually be given a much lower priority than defence and trade. These governments are likely to
be accused of 'inconsistency' in their human-rights policies,
at home and abroad, but a foreign policy dominated by military and economic priorities will almost certainly be 'inconsistent' in its concern for human rights. Governments are also
not unified actors: they consist of different ministries, subject
to different pressure groups, and these will lead to inconsistency in human-rights foreign policy. In addition, although
UN rhetoric says that human rights, peace and economic
development are interdependent, in the real world of foreign
policy, pursuing these goals consistently may not always be
possible (Baehr 1996: 1999: 84–90). The demand that the
promotion of human rights should be a dominant goal of
foreign policy is probably unrealistic, and may not be always
morally right. Nevertheless, states could probably do more
than they do now to promote human rights without damag-
ing the pursuit of other legitimate goals, and contempt for
human rights can lead to foreign-policy disasters, as the USA
learned in such countries as Iran and the Philippines. Thus,
the strict realist theory of human rights and foreign policy is
false (Donnelly 1989, 1998, 2000). More accurate is 'the
principle of limited sacrifice', which says that some states will
sometimes include human rights among their foreign-policy
concerns, but will usually be willing to pay only a limited
price for implementing them. The principle of limited sacrifice may be as important as that of state sovereignty in
limiting the effectiveness of international actions for human
rights.

The boomerang theory

Thomas Risse and his colleagues have attempted to show
how international human-rights norms have different impacts

on different societies (Risse, Ropp and Sikkink 1999). They argue that governments which violate human rights may be subject to internal and external pressures to conform with human-rights standards, and that they may respond to these pressures from instrumental or principled motives. They may consider concessions, for example, to secure trade advantages, or because they have been 'shamed' for not conforming to the principles of the international community. It is often said that many states pay only 'lip-service' to human rights. Risse and Sikkink take lip-service seriously. Governments who 'talk the talk' of human rights may find it hard not to 'walk the walk' – that is, to back words with actions – for fear of being accused of hypocrisy. If human-rights norms become institutionalized, they may become standard operating procedures (Risse and Sikkink 1999). The dynamic in this model is provided by the 'boomerang effect'. National human-rights NGOs seek transnational support that is converted into international pressure, which, under favourable conditions, strengthens the hands of the national groups. The effectiveness of the boomerang depends on world opinion, but, over time, 'norms cascades' have occurred: the influence of human-rights norms has spread and strengthened, so that now there are few hiding-places from human-rights activism (Risse and Sikkink 1999: 18, 21).

The model proposes five phases of change. The first phase consists of repression. Repressive states often seek to prevent news of human-rights violations from leaking out. The spread of such information is necessary for the activation of a human-rights response, and the move to phase two, which consists of 'denial'. This involves the denial not merely that violations took place, but also that external pressure is legitimate. Governments may be able to mobilize nationalist sentiment in their resistance to 'outside interference'. In response, external actors can mobilize a combination of material and normative pressures: economic sanctions, 'shaming' publicity, etc. Repressive governments may 'tough out' this pressure in the hope that it will not be sustained. However, if it is sustained, and even escalated, the 'target' state may enter phase three, which is that of tactical concessions. These can lead in two directions: they may create space for internal pressure-groups to bring about further change or they may 'buy off' external pressure. Risse and Sikkink believe that governments often overestimate the extent to which they can control this process, and tactical concessions may lead to 'self-entrapment', in which governments find themselves engaged in moral dialogue with external and/or internal critics (Risse and Sikkink 1999: 22–5, 28).

In the fourth phase, human-rights norms attain 'prescriptive status': governments accept them as legitimate, even though they implement them very imperfectly. They ratify human-rights covenants, institutionalize their norms in national constitutions and/or laws, and provide their citizens with remedies for violations. Although violations occur, dialogue about them takes place in terms of human rights. In phase five, compliance with international human-rights standards becomes habitual and enforced, when necessary, by the rule of law.

There is no necessary progress towards the implementation of human rights. Governments may ignore international pressures and seek to stamp out internal resistance. If they make some concessions to such pressures, they may return to repression when the pressures relax. The main factors that affect the chances of human-rights reform are: (1) the vulnerability of repressive states to external material and moral pressures; (2) the willingness of external actors to sustain these pressures; (3) the presence or absence of class-based, ethno-national or religious forces threatening the territorial integrity or the internal cohesion of the state; (4) the space available for internal NGOs; (5) the strength of the international human-rights regime and transnational NGOs; and (6) 'norm resonance' – that is, the degree of fit between international norms and national cultures (Risse and Ropp 1999).

The authors claim that their model is superior to that of realism, which cannot explain changes in human-rights policies. Some changes have not been direct consequences of state pressures; in some cases, such as that of the Philippines, internal NGO pressure changed great-power foreign policy (Risse and Sikkink 1999: 35; Risse and Ropp 1999: 268). The boomerang model may not, however, explain such changes in foreign policy as that between the policies of presidents

Carter and Reagan. The model is also said to be superior to 'modernization' theory, which has been used to explain both repression and liberalization, and therefore explains neither (Risse and Sikkink 1999: 37; Risse and Ropp 1999: 269–70). The boomerang model provides a framework for analysing human-rights change, but it does not fulfil its promise of explaining variations among different societies. Realism and modernization may be insufficient for this, and the boomerang may add a necessary dimension by relating external to internal pressures on repressive states, but we are left with something less than a full explanation of different human-rights performance in different societies.

Risse and Ropp conclude with ten lessons for human-rights practitioners.

1 Transnational human-rights NGOs have been very influential in recent years.
2 The impact of transnational NGOs is limited by the internal politics of target states, and national NGOs have to play an important role in this arena.
3 Transnational NGOs should direct their efforts both to weakening the resistance of governments to international norms and to supporting national NGOs.
4 Different strategies may be appropriate in different phases: blaming and shaming may be more effective in the repression and denial phases, and dialogue may be more effective in the later phases.
5 Moral and legal ideas are more effective in international politics than realists recognize.
6 Transnational human-rights NGOs have been correct to rely on international law, for appeals to international law play an important role in effecting human-rights change.
7 Insofar as human-rights activists have been anti-statist, they have been mistaken, for the pressure by liberal states on repressive states forms an important part of the international implementation of human rights.
8 The global implementation of human rights requires the consistent and persistent implementation of human-rights foreign policy by those states that claim to take human rights seriously.

9   Economic and other material sanctions are more likely
    to be effective in the repression and denial phases, and
    less likely to be effective in the later phases, especially
    if the target government can mobilize a nationalist
    backlash against them.
10 Dialogue or 'constructive engagement' is unlikely to
    work in the repression and denial phases, but may be
    appropriate in the later phases (Risse and Ropp 1999:
    275–8).

The national politics of human rights

The failure of Risse and his colleagues to explain variations
in respect for human rights in different societies results from
their international-relations approach, which does not pay
sufficient attention to the *internal* causes of such variations.
This requires the approaches of comparative history and
comparative political science. We saw, in chapter 5, that
Richard Claude argued that national human-rights regimes
developed gradually in France, Britain and the USA on the
basis of capitalist economies, popular social movements and
strong states. He doubted whether this could be done when,
as is widespread around the contemporary world, rapid economic development is a dominant national priority. Claude's
relative pessimism is explained partly by the fact that he was
writing during the cold war, when the international human-
rights regime was less effective than it is now.

Donnelly later clarified the relations between economic
development and human rights. He identified three trade-offs
in these relations: needs, equality and liberty. The needs
trade-off sacrificed basic needs for investment. The equality
trade-off created inequality in order to provide incentives for
economic development. The liberty trade-off restricted civil
and political rights to allow economic growth to advance
unhindered by protest. Trade-off ideology said that trade-
offs would be temporary, and that economic development
would eventually meet basic needs, diminish inequality, and
promote civil and political rights. Donnelly tested this claim
with a comparative study of Brazil and South Korea. Brazil

showed that economic development did not necessarily benefit the poor or reduce inequality. The explanation was political, not economic: the rich were powerful, and used their power to defend inequality. South Korea achieved more rapid economic growth with less inequality and a relatively good record in the protection of social and economic rights between 1960 and 1980. This refuted the hypothesis that needs and equality trade-offs were necessary for rapid economic development. South Korea's record of civil and political rights during this period was, however, very bad. Political repression commonly accompanied economic development, but it did not necessarily lead to such development. If rapid economic development tended to produce political repression, it did not follow that any particular act of oppression was necessary to development (Donnelly 1989: 163–202).

Ted Gurr sought to explain state repression by concentrating on the way that states responded to challenges. He took into account four general types of factor: (1) the nature of the challenge; (2) the nature of the state and its ideology; (3) the extent of ethnic diversity and inequality in society; and (4) the global environment. He developed numerous hypotheses about the likelihood of state repression (Gurr 1986). These point to plausible factors that cause or inhibit human-rights violations, but fail to clarify the interrelations among the factors or the dynamics of rights-violating conflicts.

Foweraker and Landman adopted a social-movement approach to the establishment of rights regimes. Social movements seek rights from the state. States may grant rights in order to increase their legitimacy. Claims for rights may, however, be counter-productive and lead to greater state repression. The social-movement approach sees rights as outcomes of struggles between subordinate groups and the state (Foweraker and Landman 1997). Whereas Gurr emphasized *state strategies* in dealing with challenges, Foweraker and Landman emphasized the social bases of struggles for rights. They neglected the international dimension of struggles for rights, but they did point out that the concept of 'rights' was well adapted to create solidarity among social groups with different and even partly incompatible interests, such as ethnic minorities and women.

The statistics of human rights

Foweraker and Landman used statistical analysis of four countries to show that social movements have generally been successful in gaining rights. Others have followed the lead of Strouse and Claude in seeking to explain human-rights violations by statistical methods. Mitchell and McCormick found that political prisoners and torture were more likely in poor countries and in countries that were involved in capitalist international trade (Mitchell and McCormick 1988). Henderson found that the less democracy prevailed, the more poverty existed, and the greater the inequality, the worse the repression. Contrary to the findings of Strouse and Claude, he found that rapid economic growth was associated with *less* repression (Henderson 1991). Poe and Tate found that poor states and military governments were more likely to violate civil and political rights in the 1980s. They also found that, where the level of democracy declines, human-rights violations increase. They found only a weak relation between wealth or economic growth rates and human-rights violations. By contrast, the threat of both external and internal war was positively linked with human-rights violations (Poe and Tate 1994).

Cingranelli and Richards sought to investigate whether or not the end of the cold war had brought improvements in human rights. One view would be that, since communist regimes were serious human-rights violators, and during the cold war both superpowers, the USA and the USSR, supported rights-violating regimes, the end of the cold war would bring considerable improvements in respect for human rights. An alternative view was that, since many violent conflicts had broken out after the end of the cold war, human-rights violations might have increased. Research had generally shown that democracy was strongly associated with human rights, so that the post-cold war increase in democracy should have led to human-rights improvements. Helen Fein, however, had found 'more murder in the middle', that is to say that what she called 'life-integrity violations' were most likely to occur in societies that lay in the middle between democracy and authoritarianism. The democratization of authoritarian political systems might, therefore, be dangerous for the protection of human rights (Fein 1995).

Cingranelli and Richards examined a random sample of seventy-nine countries in the period 1981–96. The level of respect for the rights to be protected from disappearance, extra-judicial killing and torture did not improve by a statistically significant amount. Indeed, the amount of torture in 1996 was more than it had been throughout most of the cold war. However, the level of respect for the right not to be imprisoned for political reasons nearly doubled after the end of the cold war. Almost all this improvement occurred immediately after the cold war ended (1990–93). There was no evidence of improvement in the years 1993–6. Cingranelli and Richards concluded that the strongest explanation for the reduction in political prisoners after the end of the cold war was the extent of democratization and, to a lesser extent, the increase in participation in the global economy. Neither the substantial increase in internal conflict that occurred after the end of the cold war nor inter-state conflicts in this period had a significant independent effect on respect for the right not to be imprisoned for political reasons (Cingranelli and Richards 1999). The statistical method tells us nothing about human-rights improvements and failures in particular countries, but it does paint for us a rather bleak picture of human rights after the cold war, except for the finding that more democracy means fewer political prisoners. Sabine Zanger, in a study of 147 countries from 1977 to 1993, found that violations of life-integrity rights decreased in the year of change from authoritarian to democratic government but increased in the following year. This suggests that democratization itself produces short-term benefits for these rights, but that the consolidation of democracy may be associated with violations. She also suggested that the use of economic sanctions to improve human rights may be counter-productive, since lowering a country's economic performance is more likely to worsen than improve its respect for human rights (Zanger 2000).

Milner, Poe and Leblang found that democracies score better than authoritarian states on economic and social rights, as well as on personal security. In contrast with Cingranelli and Richards, they found that human-rights performance worsened from 1989 to 1992 and improved in 1993. This difference may be the product of different statistical methods, rights studied, time-frames, and/or sample of countries. Technical differences in statistical methods can, therefore, lead to different substantive conclusions. The study also lends some support to the thesis that security, subsistence and liberty rights are indivisible and interdependent, and that the need for trade-offs is limited. This finding is preliminary, and further research is needed to test whether trade-offs can be avoided (Milner, Poe and Leblang 1999).

NGOs in world politics

These statistical studies demonstrate *relationships* between various social, economic and political factors and certain types of human-rights behaviour, but, with the exception of the study of Foweraker and Landman, which is confined to only four similar countries, they tell us little or nothing about the effects of *human-rights activism*. In recent years non-governmental organizations (NGOs) have played an increasing role in human-rights politics at local, national and international levels, and very recently the serious study of these organizations has begun.

NGOs working for human rights are not new. Following medieval religious and academic networks, the flourishing of liberal ideas in the eighteenth-century Enlightenment encouraged the founding of various humanitarian societies. A society to work for the abolition of slavery was formed in 1787, and the British and Foreign Anti-Slavery Society was formed in 1839; this, the oldest human-rights NGO in the world, exists today as Anti-Slavery International. In the nineteenth century, international societies were active in the struggle against slavery and for the emancipation of women. After the end of the First World War, the International Labour Organization encouraged the participation of NGOs in international standard-setting. NGOs played an important role in ensuring that the promotion of human rights was included in the aims of the UN and in the drafting of the Universal Declaration. Article 71 of the

UN Charter states that the Economic and Social Council 'may make suitable arrangements for consultations with non-governmental organizations which are concerned with matters within its competence.' In 1948 forty-one NGOs had consultative status with the council, in 1968 the number was 500, and in 1992 there were more than 1000 (Korey 1998). Keck and Sikkink estimate that in 1953 there were thirty-three human-rights international NGOs (INGOs), and in 1993 there were 168. In the same period, the number of development INGOs increased from three to thirty-four, and the number devoted to women's rights from ten to sixty-one (Keck and Sikkink 1998: 10–11). Edwards and Hulme identify 1600 NGOs registered in the economically developed countries in 1980, a figure that rose to 2970 in 1993. In 1909, there were 176 INGOs; in 1993, there were 28,900. In Nepal alone, 220 NGOs were registered in 1990 and 1210 in 1993. The Bangladesh Rural Advancement Committee had more than 12,000 staff in 1993. These developments have been called the 'associational revolution' (Edwards and Hulme 1996: 1–2). The organizations that took part in the early years of the UN were religious, business, trades-union and women's associations. During the cold war, NGOs were not viewed favourably by the communist or third-world states, and most international NGOs were based in the West. The very idea of independent citizens' organizations seemed to belong to the Western, liberal-democratic tradition, and was inimical to the authoritarian statism of the communist and third-world societies (Otto 1996; Korey 1998: 77).

UN human-rights institutions were suspicious of NGOs at first, but gradually made increasing use of them. NGOs publicized human-rights violations, campaigned to persuade governments to refrain from them, and played an important role in UN standard-setting and implementation procedures (Claude and Weston 1992: 11; Wiseberg 1992: 376; Cohen 1990; Brett 1995: 103–4; Clark 2001). NGOs have also played an increasingly important role in UN conferences. Baehr estimates that 1500 NGOs attended the Vienna human-rights conference of 1993 (Baehr 1999: 114, 123). Almost 3000 NGOs were accredited to the 1995 World Conference on Women (Otto 1996: 120).

NGOs range from one-person organizations to large international bodies, and from the well-intentioned amateur to the highly professional. There are international NGOs, such as Amnesty International and Human Rights Watch, national NGOs, and local NGOs, sometimes known as CBOs (community-based organizations). Some international and national organizations, such as religious bodies and trades unions, that are not primarily concerned with human rights, may play an important role in certain human-rights issues. Some of these organizations are genuinely concerned with human rights, but others may use the human-rights cause to further other aims. Some organizations that are apparently non-governmental are actually government-controlled. NGOs are neither opposition groups as such nor political parties, even though these may have genuine concerns for human rights. The greatly increased number of NGOs has given rise to problems of co-operation. There are, in particular, some tensions between Western-based NGOs, some of which are relatively long-established, professionalized and well-financed, and NGOs from poorer countries, which are less well-resourced, and may have different perspectives on human rights. These tensions are not necessarily regrettable, for they can enrich the struggle for human rights. Nevertheless, NGOs can be competitors for scarce resources, and this can distort their work (Claude and Weston 1992: 12; Baehr 1999: 114–15, 121–4).

Forsythe identifies several difficulties in measuring the influence of NGOs. They have undoubtedly made an important contribution to the development of international law and institutions, but the effectiveness of this law and these institutions is uncertain. NGOs may well have raised world consciousness about human rights, but this is difficult to measure. Forsythe does not doubt that NGOs have prevented many human-rights violations, but he believes that, because they can be 'purist' and legalistic, they are reluctant to recognize that their policies may have adverse consequences. He suggests the following kinds of success: (1) getting human-rights issues on the political agenda; (2) getting serious discussion of the issues; (3) getting procedural or institutional changes; (4) getting policy changes that improve respect for human rights. Forsythe's caution is salutary, but perhaps excessive. We cannot measure the effectiveness of NGOs precisely, but nearly everyone familiar with human-rights politics acknowledges their influence, including many governments whom they have criticized, and this suggests that the influence is significant. It is often said that NGOs work by 'the mobilization of shame' (Baehr 1999: 114). This may be misleading, however, for human-rights violators may feel little shame, but the publicity that NGOs give to the violation of international norms, which the offending governments may have supported publicly through declarations and ratification of covenants, may damage their standing in the international community. From a social-scientific point of view, states may be seen as concerned with their reputation in the community on which they depend for material and non-material benefits, and their responses to NGO pressures may be motivated by the calculation that this is in their national interest (Claude and Weston 1992: 12; Baehr 1999: 126–7; Forsythe 2000: 169, 173–7).

Perhaps the most important function of international NGOs is the provision of reliable information to governments, inter-governmental organizations, politicians, news media, academics and the general public. UN human-rights institutions are poorly resourced and very dependent on NGOs for information (Baehr 1999; Brett 1995). Governments lie. NGOs can publicize part of the truth (Brett 1995: 101–3). They may also play an important role at national level in the drafting of constitutions and human-rights law (Wiseberg 1992: 376). NGO representatives are sometimes members of official delegations, and some become governmental officials with human-rights responsibilities. NGOs seek to influence governments, but they need to maintain their independence even from relatively co-operative governments. Similarly, NGOs may welcome publicity for human-rights violations by the media, but the media can distort the global human-rights agenda.

NGOs are sometimes referred to as 'grass-roots organizations', but the extent to which they are so is highly variable, and the term is somewhat misleading. Some NGOs consist of a small elite of human-rights professionals; others combine professionals with concerned citizens; yet others have roots among the people whose rights they seek to defend. There are thousands of national and local NGOs around the world that combine human-rights, humanitarian and development programmes, providing services that their states do not provide (Claude 2002). This raises the question of the accountability of NGOs. To whom should they be accountable? Their members? Those they seek to help? Their own governments, law and/or public opinion? The governments, law and/or public opinion of countries they seek to influence? The international community? This raises also the question of the relation between the accountability and the effectiveness of NGOs (Baehr 1999: 115–24).

Another role of NGOs is to provide direct aid to the victims of human-rights violations through legal aid, medical assistance and financial support. They raise consciousness through human-rights education, which may be formal or informal, independent of or supported by governments, and narrowly legal or broadly interdisciplinary in a way that connects the concept of human rights with the practical concerns of the people (Andreopoulos and Claude 1997; Claude 2002). NGOs provide an important bridge between the remote world of law, politics and bureaucracy, on the one hand, and the actual experience of human-rights violations, on the other. Western-based NGOs can be very professional, and fairly effective, but there is a need for 'the democratization of human rights' through the empowerment of local organizations. Ironically, governments that complain of the Western bias of NGOs often prevent the formation of NGOs in their own countries (Brett 1995: 105–6). There is a considerable gap between UN institutions and genuinely grass-roots NGOs, many of which have few resources to gain access to, or assistance from these institutions (Smith, Pagnucco and Lopez 1998: 412).

Human-rights NGOs have been criticized on the ground that their assumptions and working methods are irrelevant to the most serious human-rights violations, such as the genocidal events that have taken place in Burundi, Cambodia, Bosnia and Rwanda (Korey 1998: 308–9, 312–13). There is some truth in this criticism, but it is nonetheless unfair, unless certain facts are taken into account. Firstly, NGOs have sometimes provided early warnings of human-rights disasters, and it has not been their fault that governments have failed to respond. Secondly, NGOs have been willing to adapt to changing human-rights problems: Amnesty International, for example, modified its emphasis on prisoners of conscience to campaign against 'disappearances' in the 1970s. Thirdly, NGOs have very limited resources. NGOs seek to influence governments by appearing 'non-political' and appealing to international law. This is a *politically* rational strategy for improving human rights world-wide, but it has its limits. There is room for a more robust and confrontational politics of human rights, which will also have its achievements and its limitations. In addition, human-rights NGOs have been criticized for being biased towards Western priorities and for emphasizing civil and political rights at the expense of economic, social and cultural rights. While there is truth in this criticism, it is partly misleading because NGOs concerned with development have not considered themselves to be human-rights NGOs. NGOs do play a very important role in development, however (Otto 1996: 121).

The international human-rights regime is a political as well as a legal institution. As such, it reflects the balance of power in the world. Following the end of the cold war, the balance of political and economic power is held by the West, and consequently the Western human-rights agenda dominates the international human-rights regime. NGOs with different priorities constitute a social movement that counteracts those of the major state powers, though selectively and with limited resources (Krasner 1995: 164, 167). International human-rights law has been developed to modify, but not to reject, the statist conception of international society. Some human-rights NGOs operate within that state-centred, human-rights regime; others challenge the 'club of states' as social movements with grass roots; yet others seek to form a bridge between these two very different worlds (Otto 1996).

8

Development and Globalization: Economics and Human Rights

Development *versus* human rights?

During the cold war the supposedly universal concept of human rights had to make its way in a world divided between the liberal-capitalist ideology of the West and the socialist ideology of the East. It also had to face the challenge of the newly decolonized states that accepted the concept of human rights in principle, but were very poor, and for whom 'self-determination' and 'development' were high-priority values. Under their influence, the UN General Assembly in 1974 called for a New International Economic Order (NIEO) that would address the problem of global inequality. The concept of human rights was reinterpreted by some to refer not only to the legal obligations of states to their citizens, but also to the *structural* causes of global inequality. This is one of the main concerns underlying the controversial idea of 'third-generation' rights. Third-world governments have, at least until recently, emphasized economic, social and cultural rights and marginalized civil and political rights. Western governments and human-rights activists defended the importance of civil and political rights. The view that all human rights are 'indivisible' and 'interdependent' was affirmed by a consensus of all governments in the Vienna Declaration of 1993.

The end of the cold war was a victory of liberal capitalism over authoritarian socialism, and some dramatic improvements in civil and political rights immediately took place in the former communist countries. But human rights had now to be implemented in a world dominated by global capitalism. The Western governments treated human rights and free-market economics as mutually necessary. However, even if markets are the most efficient means to produce wealth, they are not designed to protect universal economic and social rights, and it is generally agreed that, if unregulated, they fail to do so. The world's richest states have, through institutions such as the World Bank, the International Monetary Fund (IMF), the G7 (the group of the world's seven richest states) and the World Trade Organization (WTO), supported 'structural adjustment programmes' (SAPs) in poor countries that weaken the capacity of their governments to protect the economic and social rights of their poorest citizens. Thus, although the period immediately following the end of the cold war saw some important improvements in civil and political rights in many countries, protections for economic and social rights declined in many others.

Until recently, the concepts of 'human rights' and 'development' lived separate lives in UN and NGO circles, and the division between civil and political rights, on the one hand, and economic and social rights, on the other, was maintained. This division was often associated with the view that 'development' was a *precondition* of respect for human rights in accordance with the slogan 'bread first, freedom later'. We have seen, however, that rapid economic development can be associated with respect for economic and social rights, and also with the violation of civil and political rights, as in South Korea and Taiwan, but that most so-called developmental dictatorships fail to deliver development. The relationship between economic development and human rights is still not well understood but is almost certainly complex, not least because the concepts of 'human rights' and 'development' have various meanings.

Robert Goodin has reviewed several of the most common (and apparently plausible) arguments for the proposition that development requires the restriction of human rights. The first is that respect for economic and social rights transfers resources from savings, investment and capital accumulation, and thereby slows down economic development. A second is that democratic politics favour special interests at the expense of the national economy. A version of these two arguments says that trades-union rights favour consumption over investment, and thereby slow economic growth. Another argument is that civil rights reduce the capacity of the government to control crime and thereby hinder development. A version of this is that the restriction of civil and political rights enables governments to create social stability, which attracts foreign investment and which in turn contributes to economic development. Goodin argues, to the contrary, that respect for economic and social rights – such as health, education and jobs – may be an investment in human capital, while the rich do not necessarily spend their wealth on productive investment. Democratic politics may distort economic development, but so does corruption in authoritarian systems. Respect for human rights may reduce workers' unrest. It is doubtful whether the violation of civil rights reduces crime, and more doubtful whether it promotes economic growth. Democratic regimes may provide a more stable environment for foreign investment. Goodin adds that authoritarian regimes divert considerable resources from development to repression (Goodin 1979).

Amartya Sen maintains that the evidence suggests little correlation, positive or negative, between respect for civil and political rights and economic growth, and that the violation of such rights is not *necessary* to economic development. Political authoritarianism is not the *cause* of economic growth. In contrast, civil and political rights hold governments accountable to prevent disasters such as famines. Civil and political rights therefore have an *instrumental* value in securing governmental policies favourable to development and human rights, and they also have an *intrinsic* value in recognizing human dignity. Sen adds that human rights are necessary to the *conceptualization* of what economic needs are. The fact that the meaning of 'development' is contested is itself a reason for protecting civil and political rights in order to democratize development strategies (Sen 1999).

Zehra Arat argues that the protection of economic and social rights is necessary to the protection of civil and political rights in developing countries. Inegalitarian development undermines the legitimacy of developmental regimes, and this leads to authoritarianism. Since unregulated capitalism tends strongly to be inegalitarian, unregulated capitalist development is not likely to lead to the protection of human rights (Arat 1991).

The idea that human rights must be 'traded off' for development has so often failed to produce development that the once-fashionable trade-off theory has been replaced by an emphasis on 'good governance', which, although concerned with economic efficiency rather than human rights, is friendlier towards human rights than was the idea of trade-off.

The 'good-governance' ideology is associated with the view that governments should provide democracy (at least in the form of free and fair elections) and respect civil and political rights, and leave development largely to market forces. This makes the protection of economic and social rights very difficult. It has also turned the attention of human-rights activists and scholars to the question of the responsibility of private economic actors – especially multinational corporations (MNCs) – for human rights. Many MNCs are richer and more powerful than most states: of the world's one hundred biggest economies, forty-nine are states and fifty-one are corporations. Although there are well-documented cases of MNCs violating human rights, we lack systematic evidence of their record. The international trade regime represented by the WTO is not designed to protect human rights, and attempts to integrate the global trade and human-rights regimes have been very weak (Forsythe 2000: 19, 191, 195–6, 199; McCorquodale and Fairbrother 1999).

The right to development

In the 1960s the newly independent states argued that formal independence and the legal equality of states had little value without a more equitable distribution of the world's economic resources. In 1972, Keba M'Baye, a senior Senegalese judge, argued in a public lecture that everyone had the right to development, 'the right to live better'. As chairman of the

Human Rights Commission, M'Baye was instrumental in the adoption in 1977 of a resolution that the UN undertake a study of the right to development as a human right. Within three years, the right to development had been proclaimed as a human right by the General Assembly, and in 1986 the assembly adopted its Declaration on the Right to Development (Rich 1988).

The original formulation suggested that the right was an individual human right, but it came to be interpreted as both an individual and a collective right. This raised questions as to who had the corresponding obligations, and what they had obligations to do. The conventional answer would be that states had the obligations. The discourse of the right to development has implied, however, that rich countries have the obligation to help poor countries to develop, although the precise nature of this obligation has remained unclear and controversial. It is also unclear and controversial whether the right to development is a distinct human right or a summary of several other human rights (Espiell 1981; Donnelly 1985b: 474–5).

Donnelly has argued that there is no right to development. The development of individuals, he maintains, is the goal and justification of all human rights. Some have argued that the right to development is an elaboration of Article 22 of the Universal Declaration, which says that everyone is entitled to realization 'through national effort and international co-operation' of his economic, social and cultural rights. Donnelly doubts whether the supposed right to development is an advance, conceptually or practically, on Article 22. He also rejects the argument that the right to development is required by international justice. He argues that human rights are derived from the fact of being human and not from conceptions of justice. Barry agrees that the right to development is worthless, but argues that it should be *replaced by* a conception of global justice (Barry 2000). It is not clear, however, why there cannot be a human right to economic justice, although theories of justice are notoriously controversial, and it may well be that they can help neither to clarify nor to implement the right to development. Donnelly also objects to the right to development, because it is partly a collective right, and collective rights are not human rights 'as that term is ordinarily understood' (Donnelly 1985b: 497–8). Donnelly's argument is incoherent here, because his 'social constructivist' approach to human rights must recognize that the right to development has been socially constructed as a collective human right. This may show that social constructivism is flawed rather than that the right to development deserves our support, for what is socially constructed may be unclear, incoherent and/or dangerous. Donnelly concludes that the supposed right to development either adds nothing to established human rights or provides a dangerous excuse for violating them. There is very little solid evidence that the introduction of this right has done much harm or much good, and so the debate over the right has been inconclusive.

Globalization

The idea of the New International Economic Order has been swept away in recent years by the concept of 'globalization'. The concept is multi-dimensional (economic, cultural, political, military and social), but economic globalization has dominated recent debates, and this is closely associated with the ideology of neo-liberalism, which favours free markets and reduced governmental intervention in economic affairs. In this form, globalization weakens the international human-rights regime insofar as that regime imposes obligations on states to implement human rights, including economic and social rights, and neo-liberalism is opposed to strong states. This has led to some incoherence in 'the international community', as UN human-rights agencies continue to hold states responsible for human-rights implementation, while financial institutions, such as the IMF, require governments to implement policies that make it more difficult for them to protect the human rights, especially the social and economic rights, of their citizens. Recently, attempts have been made through the UN Development Programme, to some extent the World Bank, and to a lesser extent the IMF, to integrate international development and human-rights policies, but these attempts have so far been quite weak. Human-rights activists have put considerable faith in NGOs, but there is a concern that the displacement of responsibility from relatively strong and well-resourced, though often corrupt states, to well-intentioned, sometimes very professional and effective, but relatively under-resourced NGOs, may weaken the international human-rights project, especially with respect to economic and social rights. Globalization has drawn more women world-wide into the labour force, but women feature disproportionately among the most exploited workers. This has led to what has been called 'the feminization of poverty'. Women are under-represented in global economic decision-making bodies and over-represented among the victims of globalization. *Globalization is gendered* (Oloka-Onyango and Udagama 2000).

David Held and his colleagues propose a more radical conception of globalization. Although they recognize that state sovereignty is still an important element of international politics, they see globalization as a dynamic form of power which is transforming the structure of the world that is taken for granted by international law, including international human-rights law. Consequently key concepts of the international human-rights regime, such as state sovereignty and self-determination, are being undermined by forces that sweep across state borders, showing only contempt for the principle of the territorial integrity of states. Nevertheless, on this account, the international human-rights regime is itself a form of globalization, and thus we cannot say that globalization is simply bad for human rights (Held et al. 1999: 8–9, 28–31).

The myth of international law is that the world is divided into sovereign, independent states. It is not, and never has been. In the era of European imperialism, the spread of imperial power expressed the sovereignty of the imperial states, while it denied sovereignty to colonized peoples. Imperialism was, however, a system not only of state power but also of powerful private economic organizations (the early multinational corporations) and cultural entrepreneurs (e.g., missionaries). With the increase of global political and economic reach, and the accompanying development of trans-state technologies, the *international regime* was born to co-ordinate these activities – the International Telegraph Union (1865) being the first. The novelty of the international human-rights regime established after the Second World War was that it introduced a new principle for the *legitimation* of states with a strong potential for clashing with the traditional principle of state sovereignty. Consequently, the concept of human rights belongs both to the traditional international legal discourse of the sovereign state and to the discourse of globalization that threatens to subvert it. In the world that globalization has made, sovereign states are still powerful actors, but they share the world with multinational corporations, international regimes and international NGOs. One field in which economic considerations are undermining state sovereignty, with important implications for human rights, is the production and exchange of military technology, as the familiar term 'the arms trade' suggests. World government, once the ideal of some cosmopolitan liberals, is now widely considered neither possible nor desirable, but increasing concern for human rights, trans-state environmental problems, international crime, health issues (e.g., HIV/AIDS) and migration has introduced the concept of 'global governance'. In this way both the concepts of state sovereignty and human rights have been drawn into a complex global system which the traditional statist model of international law maps rather inadequately. States and their legal systems are involved in a global legal and extra-legal system (Held et al. 1999).

The UN system is based on the sovereignty of states, but it has global aims, such as peace, the regulation of the global economy through such institutions as the World Bank and the IMF, human rights and development, as well as the control of crime and various forms of technical regulation. Although it is a system of power, unlike the 'classical' system of state sovereignty it is not a system of naked power, but it is highly moralized, especially by the human-rights idea. The Nuremberg trials of Nazi war criminals after the Second World War assumed both that the 'international community' could hold states accountable for 'crimes against humanity' and that individuals could have obligations to an authority higher than that of the state. International human-rights law is, therefore, both statist, since states are the primary bearers of human-rights obligations, and supra-statist, since states can be held accountable by supra-state bodies (Held et al. 1999: 62, 72, 74).

The problems of development, and of economic and social rights, have to be addressed in a world in which sovereign states have to act in a complex environment that limits their power. Economic globalization has distributed its benefits very unevenly: East Asia has done much better, for example, than sub-Saharan Africa. There is a widespread perception that the recent phase of globalization has increased competition among states, and that this has in turn eroded the welfare state, and thereby economic and social rights, even in the richest countries. But it is controversial whether welfare budgets in rich countries have really declined, and, even if they have, whether globalization is the *cause* of their decline or an *excuse* for politicians who wished to cut them for ideological reasons. What is certain is that those who wish to maintain the welfare state in the twenty-first century must do so in the context of a globalized economy and international trading regimes such as that supervised by the WTO. Many people believe that global *financial* transactions are more difficult to regulate than international trade, but Held and his colleagues point out that states regulate financial institutions within their jurisdictions, and global institutions are able to regulate international finance if they have the will to do so. Global finance is nevertheless market-driven, and the dynamics of global financial markets produce a very difficult environment for the implementation of economic and social rights (Held et al. 1999).

There are international regimes regulating global trade and finance, even though they may not be very favourable to human rights, but there is no international regime regulating multinational corporations as such. The dominant neo-liberal ideology has meant that developing countries are now more open than ever to foreign direct investment (FDI) by MNCs. This is endorsed by the World Bank and reinforced by the WTO's trade regime. Developing countries, in order to attract foreign investment, come under pressure not only to reduce public expenditure for economic and social rights, but also to reduce the burden on MNCs in such areas as workplace safety and environmental protection. Some commentators emphasize that MNCs are subject to regulation in their 'home' states; others that MNCs are 'footloose' and can move to wherever the living is easiest for them – that is, where costs are lowest. MNCs can be regulated to some extent, but their relative mobility means that they have considerable autonomy both from their 'home' governments and from the governments of countries in which they invest, and from which they can fairly easily disinvest. It is wrong to assume that the impact of MNCs is always harmful to human rights, for they may create jobs and wealth, but they are not in the business of human rights, and they have sometimes been involved in serious human-rights violations (Held et al. 1999).

Cingranelli and Richards have attempted to test the relations between capitalism and human rights statistically. They suggest that increases in foreign direct investment in developing countries are significantly associated with increases in governmental respect for civil and political rights. They found that, apart from the degree of post-cold war democratization, only the degree of participation in the global economy had a statistically significant effect on pre- and post-cold war changes in governmental policies towards political prisoners (Cingranelli and Richards 1999). Mitchell and McCormick, however, found a positive association between, on the one hand, trade between capitalist and third-world countries, and, on the other hand, political prisoners and the use of torture (Mitchell and McCormick 1988). Davenport found no relation between economic dependency and repression (Davenport 1996).

William Meyer has investigated the question as to whether private corporations violate or improve human rights in the third world through a study of US corporations. He points out that the neo-liberal global economic ideology does not simply originate from international financial institutions (IFIs) but is partly a product of US foreign policy, which operates through 'soft' economic power as much as 'hard' military power: Microsoft and McDonalds may have more impact on the world than US nuclear weapons. The collapse of the communist model of economic development has led the less developed countries to look to capitalist models of development in the hope that MNCs would bring investment and jobs, and thereby reduce poverty. Meyer's statistical study found that foreign direct investment (FDI) was positively associated with civil and political rights as well as with economic and social rights in the third world. FDI was positively associated with increased life expectancy, reduced infant mortality, employment and reduction in illiteracy. Meyer concluded that capitalist MNCs are 'engines of development' that promote civil and political rights and socio-economic welfare. Globally, there is a positive relation between MNC investment in the third world and human rights. This conclusion is consistent with evidence of human-rights violations by particular MNCs in particular third-world countries (Meyer 1996; 1998).

Bruce Moon, using different methods, found that the presence of multinational corporations was associated with lower levels of meeting basic needs. He concluded that basic-needs improvements do not slow economic growth; indeed, states with relatively good basic-needs achievements grow more rapidly than under-achievers (Moon 1991). Smith, Bolyard and Ippolito argue that Meyer's inclusion of only US MNCs makes his test of the impact of MNCs on human rights too limited. Using a different method, they found that FDI was either negatively related or unrelated to human rights (Smith, Bolyard and Ippolito 1999). Meyer responded by pointing out that, since the two studies used different methods, the second did not contradict the first. The two studies together show that, at the cross-national level, the evidence linking MNCs to human rights is mixed. At the level of case studies, the evidence is also mixed. This leaves room for the media and NGOs to campaign for improved human-rights performance by particular MNCs with some hope of success (Meyer 1999).

Activists have mobilized consumers, shareholders, investors, and even local government authorities against MNCs involved in human-rights violations. In doing this, activists are bypassing states in foreign policy-making, contrary to the assumptions of the realist theory of international relations. Such actions may play a significant part in world politics: for example, private bank sanctions on the apartheid regime in South Africa had an important impact on its fall. Corporations can be influenced by 'the hassle factor': consumers and shareholders can divert sufficient resources to dealing with their campaigns that it becomes cheaper to give in than to fight. Human-rights NGOs have, therefore, somewhat altered the perception by MNCs of what both their interests and their obligations are. The limits of these actions are set by the fact that MNCs are motivated by self-interest, not by human rights as such, and the international trade regime of the WTO has the promotion of trade, and not of human rights, as its overriding objective (Rodman 1998).

The UN and other international organizations, such as Amnesty International, have attempted to get MNCs to adopt corporate human-rights codes of conduct, with varying, but generally limited, success. In the 1990s many major retailers and clothing corporations adopted policies on forced labour, child labour, trades-unions rights, employment discrimination, health and safety, and, in some cases, minimum wages and maximum hours. Some MNCs have pulled out of rights-violating countries such as China and Burma/Myanmar. Some 800 firms have formed an association called Business for Social Responsibility with a programme on human rights. It has been estimated, however, that fewer than 10 per cent of US-based MNCs have human-rights codes. The recognition by MNCs that they have human-rights obligations has, therefore, made some, rather limited progress (Cassel 1996). In January 1999, the UN Secretary-General, Kofi Annan, proposed a 'global compact' for MNCs. This is a voluntary agreement by which MNCs undertake to abide by nine human-rights and environmental principles. Some important MNCs have signed up to this, and some specific initiatives have been started. The Global Compact will be a good test of the relative merits of the 'structuralist' view that global capitalism is necessarily hostile to human rights and the 'idealist' or 'voluntarist' view that, where there is the will, there is a way to improve human rights. The compact is a public commitment by MNCs to international human-rights standards, and thereby helps to make them more accountable (United Nations 2001; Claude 2002).

It is sometimes assumed that 'globalization' is simply bad for human rights (Schwab and Pollis 2000: 215–16). The human-rights regime and the human-rights movement are, however, parts of cultural, legal and political globalization. Cultural globalization and its supporting technological infrastructure (satellite TV, internet, etc.) carry human-rights ideas around the world, as they also carry ideas hostile to human rights, such as racism and religious fanaticism. McGrew has suggested that the global human-rights movement has, paradoxically, not been wholly favourable to human rights, because it has privileged the human-rights concepts of the West and provoked illiberal reactions to Western hegemony (McGrew 1998: 205). This dialectic between human rights and its critics is certainly a feature of cultural globalization, but it is hard to see how it is, on the whole, other than beneficial for human rights. It is good that Western conceptions of human rights are challenged, although some of the challenges are very bad for human rights. Further, the concept of human rights is not only a global concept, globally diffused, but it requires global institutions for its implementation. The human-rights movement is a global social movement that presupposes a global moral community. It operates, however, in a world in which nation-states, MNCs and particularistic forces hostile to human rights exercise considerable power. The concept of human rights is inextricably bound up with globalization in complex ways, and the task of human-rights thinkers and activists is not to denounce globalization, but to understand it, and learn how to act effectively within it (Held et al. 1999; McCorquodale and Fairbrother 1999).

International financial institutions

In 1944, as the Second World War drew to its close, the allies met at the United Nations Monetary and Financial Conference in Bretton Woods, New Hampshire, to address the world's economic problems. The main outcomes of these deliberations were the World Bank, the International Monetary Fund, and the General Agreement on Tariffs and Trade (GATT), which has recently been transformed into the World Trade Organization. Collectively, these are known as the Bretton Woods institutions, and they constitute a global economic regime (Cleary 1996: 63). These international financial institutions (IFIs) have as their goals economic stability and development, not the promotion or protection of human rights. Their operations are governed by global economic forces and prevailing economic ideologies, and not by human-rights ideals. This gap between economic considerations and human-rights principles has been aggravated by the fact that, until recently, IFIs not only neglected human rights, but affirmed that their commitment to 'non-political' economic policies *required* them to ignore human rights. This led to an important form of incoherence within the UN system and the 'international community', in that global economic strategies were developed not only separately from human-rights strategies, but often in ways that were harmful to human rights. This was particularly true for the structural adjustment programmes (SAPs) for developing countries and the protection of economic and social rights. A number of developing countries with vulnerable sections of the population who suffered from the imposition of SAPs experienced 'IMF riots' in the 1970s and 1980s (Samson 1992: 665–6; Cleary 1996: 75).

The tension within the UN system is that it is supposed to promote the common good of humanity while respecting the sovereign rights of states. The IFIs, as originally constructed, respected the principle of state sovereignty in two ways: (1) only states could participate in their work; (2) they were required to respect the sovereignty of states in carrying out their mandates. However, states that seek the assistance of the World Bank and the IMF have to accept conditions that limit their autonomy and erode their sovereignty. Poor states are obviously much more vulnerable than rich states to financial intervention by IFIs. The statist assumptions of the UN and the IFIs have been undermined, however, by the realities of globalization. Poverty is not merely a social and economic problem for sovereign states. It can also be a cause of conflict that in turn produces state repression and refugee flows. Thus, economic and financial problems are connected to human-rights problems, which cross the territorial borders of states. Insofar as the 'international community' is fixated on the principle of the territorial integrity of states, it is losing touch with human-rights realities. Human-rights NGOs have, however, also, until recently, neglected the connections between civil and political rights, on the one hand, and economic and social rights, on the other, and the place of human rights in the fields of economics, poverty, trade, investment and environmental degradation. There are many explanations of this: limited resources; desire for a clear image; desire to avoid unnecessary controversy; fear of allowing lack of development to be used as an excuse for oppression; human-rights legalism; and a failure of Western culture to integrate philosophy, law, politics and economics. No two fields have been so closely interrelated in practice, but so separated conceptually, as development economics and human rights (Bradlow and Grossman 1995: 413–20; Cleary 1996: 76).

Both the World Bank and the IMF have broadened their interpretation of their mandates in recognition of the close interrelations among issues of development, human rights and the environment. The IMF has taken some account of the structural causes of international debt and underdevelopment, and this at least opens the door to a consideration of human rights. The World Bank, confronting the failure of many development projects, has turned its attention to the social conditions of development. In so doing, it has intruded further into state sovereignty and opened itself up to non-state actors, for example NGOs. It has adopted a new information-disclosure policy, an Independent Inspection Panel to hear complaints about its procedures from affected private parties, and an NGO–World Bank Committee in which NGO representatives and World Bank officials meet regularly to discuss matters of mutual concern. There have even been exchanges of personnel between the bank and NGOs. The NGOs that participate in these discussions have, however, been criticized for their lack of accountability and for legitimating questionable activities of the bank. NGO influence on the bank can lead to resistance from the borrowing state (Fox 2000). The IMF has more limited dialogue with private actors but does hold informal discussions with both MNCs and NGOs.

The power of IFIs is considerable, and their legal obligations are few. They are, however, part of the international legal order, and, as such, they ought to have human-rights obligations. They now advocate 'good governance' (including transparency and popular participation) for client-states, but have been criticized for not practising it themselves. The World Bank has reinterpreted its mandate to include some human-rights problems, but it has done this in an ad hoc way, and still excludes some human-rights issues from consideration on the ground that they are 'political'. It is not consistent about this, however, since it has sometimes acted, under pressure, in a clearly political manner, for example by curtailing loans to socialist Chile and Islamic Iran. It has also, on some occasions, under pressure from powerful states, delayed, withdrawn, blocked or redirected loans as a result of serious human-rights concerns (Forsythe 1997). As states often violate human rights from political motives, so IFIs violate human rights from economic motives. However, whereas human-rights activists have targeted states as human-rights violators, they have paid less attention to IFIs than they ought to have done. Human-rights NGOs have been too much in love with law and too afraid of economics (Bradlow and Grossman 1995; Cleary 1996).

It is widely agreed that the Bretton Woods institutions have a poor human-rights record. There is less agreement on what should be done about this. Solutions range from dialogue and reform through radical transformation to abolition. IFIs now attract the hostility that was once directed against 'capitalism', but the protests are based less on socialism than on a range of human-rights, development and environmental concerns, and the protesters are not organized political parties and revolutionary organizations, but a looser, transnational movement. There is now more co-operation between the World Bank and NGOs, but this has left as problematic the relations between these 'elite' NGOs and genuine grass-roots, community-based organizations (sometimes called GROs or CBOs) (Cleary 1996). Caroline Thomas has argued that IFIs are not so much the cause of the increasing inequalities in the world, but key actors in a global system dominated by the neo-liberal ideology that holds that markets, not states, are engines of progress for everyone, including the poorest. This ideology is refuted by the fact that the world's poorest are getting poorer, and attempts by IFIs to incorporate concern for them into their programmes have had little effect. Neo-liberalism, Thomas maintains, ignores the important role that the state has played in the remarkable economic development of certain East Asian countries, and the fact that relative equality and successful economic development can go together. Economic globalization is increasing inequality, feeding resentment, fuelling conflict, and thereby threatening the human rights that the international community claims to be promoting (Thomas 1998). One observer of the UN-sponsored peace process in El Salvador commented that the country was like a patient undergoing two simultaneous operations: the political arm of the UN was attempting to construct peace, while the IFIs were undermining it by insisting on neo-liberal economic policies that would create greater inequality (Patrick 2000: 78).

Economic and social rights

The obligations of states with respect to economic and social rights are not clear. The International Covenant on Economic, Social and Cultural Rights imposes on each state party the obligation 'to take steps, individually and through international assistance and co-operation, . . . to the maximum of its available resources, with a view to achieving progressively the full realization of the rights recognized in the present Covenant by all appropriate means.' This has been interpreted to mean that states are obliged to take immediate, deliberate, concrete and targeted steps towards the realization of these rights. They are required to ensure the satisfaction of, at the very least, minimum essential levels of these rights. They must strive for the widest possible enjoyment of the rights with particular emphasis on vulnerable members of society (Hunt, P. 1996). Bård-Anders Andreassen and his colleagues suggested a 'minimum threshold' approach, using indicators that measure nutrition, infant mortality, frequency of disease, life expectancy, income, unemployment and food consumption (Andreassen et al. 1988). This is similar to the approach of the human development index used by the UN (United Nations Development Programme 2001). Eide argues that the obligations of governments to fulfil economic and social rights must be context-dependent to a considerable degree, and that the implementation of these rights must be quite pragmatic (Eide 1989). Some implementation of economic and social rights has been carried out by UN specialized agencies, such as the International Labour Organization and the World Health Organization. The UN was slow to set up a committee to monitor compliance with the covenant, and, when it did, NGO participation in its work has been slight.

It is sometimes said that economic and social rights can be contrasted with civil and political rights because economic and social rights are not 'justiciable' – that is, cannot be decided in courts of law. This distinction is dubious, however: it is no more difficult for a court to determine whether an individual has enough food than whether she has had a fair trial (Eide 1989). The UN Committee on Economic, Social and Cultural Rights has identified some rights that could be implemented by legal institutions: equal rights for men and women; equal pay for equal work; the right to form and join trades unions and the right to strike; the right to free compulsory primary education; the right to choose a non-public school; the right to establish schools; and freedom for scientific research and creative activity. Rights to social security can be adjudicated in specialist tribunals; industrial tribunals can hear labour disputes, as housing tribunals can decide disputes relating to the right to shelter. Thus, economic, social and cultural rights can be rendered justiciable to a considerable extent. Whether the legal approach to their implementation is the best is debatable (Hunt, P. 1996: 26–9). There are two kinds of objection to the legal approach. The first is that some of the rights are specified in an objectionable way that may involve violations of other rights: the right to private education, for example, is open to the objection that it creates unequal opportunities. The second objection is that, to transfer such matters from politics to the law is anti-democratic. This objection is a special case of the general objection to taking rights out of politics. Those who believe that there are human, economic, social and cultural rights must also believe that they require institutional protection. Whether legal institutions are the best for this purpose cannot be generally stated with any confidence.

The 'classical' view was that governments or, in international law, states were responsible for the implementation of human rights. There has been a widespread belief that the implementation of economic and social rights required strong states that might be more likely to violate civil and political rights. We now know that such states can sometimes implement economic and social rights quite effectively, but usually they do not. There is now a widespread belief that free markets will do a better job. It is clear that unregulated markets will almost certainly not. Since neither states nor markets can generally be trusted to protect these rights, the social-movement, NGO-based approach may now seem the most promising. There is no doubt that NGOs can play a significant role, but there are limits to that role in the limited resources and problematic accountability of NGOs. Economic and social rights are still rather marginalized in the human-rights field, but perhaps a little less than they used to be. This reflects the marginalization of those whose rights have been most seriously violated (Hunt, P. 1996). In the era of globalization, the struggle for economic and social rights is likely to become increasingly important. This struggle will be hard, because the political and economic forces opposed to it are powerful. However, the failure of this struggle will not only be unjust. It will almost certainly fuel the persistent violent conflicts that afflict many parts of the world, and that are associated with gross violations of civil and political rights.

9
Conclusion: Human Rights in the Twenty-First Century

Learning from history

The concept of human rights is now so familiar that we need to remember how new it is. It is true that, according to some scholars, the concept of rights was implicit in ancient cultures: the commandment 'thou shalt not steal', for example, they say, implies the right to property. Other scholars, however, maintain that legal disputes in classical Greece were decided by reference to the common good rather than to the rights of the parties. Fred Miller has nevertheless made a strong case that the concept of *citizens' rights*, especially rights to political participation and property, is found in the political philosophy of Aristotle (Miller, F. 1995). The Stoic philosophers had the concept of universal natural law, but not of natural rights. It was not until the Middle Ages that, within the framework of Christian theology, the concept of universal natural rights could emerge.

There is another way of thinking about the history of the concept of human rights in different cultures. At the core of *our* concept of human rights is the idea of protecting individuals (and perhaps groups) from *the abuse of power*. All human societies have power structures, and many of them have throughout history had some conception of the abuse of power. The concepts of *natural rights* and *human rights* are particular ways of expressing this concern about the abuse of power.

It is often said that the origin of the concept of human rights can be found in the ideology with which the bourgeoisie in seventeenth-century England defended their *property interests* against the feudal class and/or absolute monarchs (Donnelly 1989: 89, 104–5). This account is inaccurate, however, for Tierney has shown that the concept of natural rights can be found centuries earlier in medieval thought (Tierney 1997). Medieval law was certainly much concerned with property, but more with land than with bourgeois property, and not all medieval conceptions of rights were directly linked with property. The Magna Carta, for example, provides for the right to a fair trial. Medieval Christian natural-rights theory was concerned with, among other things, the right to *subsistence*. Medieval debates were conducted in Latin, and, in Latin, the concept of 'property' refers to what is one's own, and that may include one's life and liberty. We see this late-medieval conception of rights in the political philosophy of John Locke, who was the first modern natural-rights thinker, but influenced by medieval conceptions of natural rights. This more complex history of the origins of modern rights theory is relevant to human-rights debates today, because it shows that talk of 'three generations' of rights is unhistorical, and that the distinction between civil and political rights, on the one hand, and economic and social rights, on the other, cannot be derived from the history of the concept, which was concerned first with the right to subsistence and other (economic) property rights, and then with civil and political rights, because these were thought to be necessary to secure the basic rights to survival and property. There are *analytical* arguments for and against distinguishing these two types of human rights today, but the historical appeal to three generations of rights is false.

There was, however, no systematic theory of natural rights until the seventeenth century. Whether this concept was 'bourgeois' is controversial, because the concept 'bourgeois' is not precise; the facts are complex; and the interpretation of theories such as Locke's is still disputed. What is more certain is that the concept of natural rights in the seventeenth and eighteenth centuries was associated with (1) opposition to absolute monarchy; (2) emergent capitalism; and (3) dissident Protestantism or secularized political thought. These themes burst onto the stage of world history in the English Revolution of 1642–9 and the American and French revolutions of the late eighteenth century.

The violent disorder of the French Revolution provoked a strong *philosophical* reaction that targeted the concept of natural rights as (a) subversive, and (b) unscientific. The concept of natural rights derived the natural rights of individuals from the supposed will of God and the belief that *reason* could tell us what was right and wrong. The scientific philosophy of the eighteenth and nineteenth centuries undermined the concept of the natural rights of individuals and replaced it with that of the science of society (sociology). Saint-Simon, Comte, Marx, Weber and Durkheim were the leaders of this development. Rights were no longer fundamental moral ideas to regulate political life, but *ideological* products of social struggle or social morality. The social sciences marginalized the concept of rights. When the United Nations, after the Second World War, revived the eighteenth-century concept of the Rights of Man as *human rights* in order to express its liberal-democratic opposition to Fascism, it ignored this social-scientific tradition. Both the concept of human rights and the social sciences have flourished since 1945, but for the most part independently of each other. Recently, the increasing influence of the concept of human rights in international and national politics, especially since the end of the cold war, has made some social scientists aware of the fact that they have ignored a major social development of the past fifty years. At last, they are applying their distinctive concepts, theories and methods to the real world of human rights and their violation. I have, in this book, offered a review, both sympathetic and critical, of the new social science of human rights in the hope that it will advance the reconciliation of ethical idealism and scientific realism that the academic study of human rights requires.

After the adoption of the Universal Declaration of Human Rights by the UN General Assembly in 1948, the slow process of standard-setting (international human-rights law) and institution-building began. The cold war blocked progress for human rights, however, as communist regimes perpetrated gross violations of civil and political rights and the West was implicated in massive violations, either directly or through support of anti-communist dictatorships. World-wide de-colonization brought many new states into the UN, paying lip-service to human rights, but with different priorities, such as economic development, anti-colonialism and anti-racism. Most had terrible records in the violation of civil and political rights, and few were successful in protecting economic and social rights. Anti-racism was, in principle, common ground among the Western, the communist and the third-world states, and the international campaign against apart-heid established the principle that human-rights violations within one nation-state were properly the object of scrutiny, condemnation and sanctions by the international community. This is still a controversial idea, resisted by many states, but it has become well established in international law and politics.

The progress of human rights since 1948 has a number of significant landmarks: the foundation of Amnesty International in 1961; the two UN covenants of 1966; the Helsinki Accord of 1975, which put human-rights pressure on the communist bloc; the human-rights foreign policy of President Jimmy Carter in the 1970s; the democratization of various Latin American and European countries (Portugal, Spain and Greece) from the mid-1980s; and the Vienna conference of 1993. The end of the cold war at the end of the 1980s produced contradictory results: liberalization in many former communist societies, but violent ethno-nationalist conflict in many others. By the end of the twentieth century the concept of human rights had become a 'hegemonic ideology'; there had been a tremendous expansion of human-rights law and institutions; there had been great real advances in many countries; and there were many unsolved political problems in the world that still gave rise to grave human-rights violations. Only six years before the century ended, more than half a million citizens of Rwanda were murdered by their government in a state-sponsored genocide. The battle for human rights was far from won.

Human rights may seem like an idea whose time has come, but this proposition must be treated with caution. We should not accept the extreme idealist view that human rights is a concept with enormous power in international politics: states still resist human-rights pressures from within and outside their societies when they think that their interests are threatened. We should not, however, take the extreme realist view that the concept of human rights makes no significant difference to international politics. Communist human-rights violations may have been brought to an end because the West won the cold war, but the concept of human rights played a role in that war. The social sciences can clarify the respective roles of ideas and material interests in the politics of human rights.

Some critics believe that the concept of human rights is too *individualistic* and *legalistic*, so that the *structural* causes of human-rights violations, especially of economic and social rights, are ignored (Evans 2001). This view almost certainly underestimates the achievements of the human-rights movement based on human-rights law, even though we do not know how to measure these achievements precisely. The structural approach is nevertheless useful in emphasizing the role played by inequalities of political power and the dynamics of the global economy in the causation of human-rights violations. It is limited by the difficulty of identifying alternative structures that would better protect human rights and are attainable. States, international institutions and multinational corporations are the principal players in international politics. NGOs have played an increasingly important role, but their resources and power are relatively weak. The UN is seriously under-funded. Its weakness can be explained by *the principle of limited sacrifice*. We are human and decent, and so we say that everyone ought to enjoy their human rights. However, human-rights declarations are cheap, whereas human-rights implementation is rather expensive. We are unwilling to pay the bill. We are disappointed at the gap between human-rights ideals and human-rights realities, but we are unwilling to recognize our fault in creating that gap, and find it easier to blame economic structures or supposedly ineffective institutions such as the UN. The weakness of the structural approach is that it fails to locate sources of possible change. The strength of the activist approach is that it emphasizes that we are responsible for the structures that we support. Human-rights activists have, however, begun to tackle the structural sources of human-rights violations (MNCs and IFIs), and so the idealist and structuralist approaches may be converging.

The history of the concept of human rights supports the contemporary thesis that human rights are 'indivisible' in that basic human material interests are closely connected with political freedom. Although the history of the concept is Western, the concept itself is universal. This history shows, too, that the concept reaches for the fundamental conditions of human well-being while evolving in response to changing social conditions. The social constructivist theory of human rights advocated by Donnelly emphasizes the changing nature of human rights (Donnelly 1985a: 87). The social sciences can explain these changes, although their achievements in doing so have so far been disappointing. Social constructivism, however, gives us no standard for *evaluating* these changes. The legacy of the history of the concept of human rights is confusion about how ethical, analytical and explanatory approaches are related to each other. Historically, social science attempted, but failed, to replace the ethical approach to human rights. Reconciling the ethics and social science of human rights is a principal challenge of the future.

Objections to human rights

The history of human rights teaches us not only that the concept of human rights is controversial, but also rather precisely *why* it is. The principal criticisms that were made in the late eighteenth and early nineteenth centuries of the Rights of Man still bite today. Burke said that the concept ignored the value of national traditions. Bentham argued that it ignored the social nature of moral and legal concepts. Marx complained that it concealed and legitimated exploitative and oppressive social structures. Such arguments are still made today. There is a danger that the success of the concept can induce complacency and dogmatism. In the face of relativist objections to human-rights universalism for being 'imperialistic', human-rights advocates would do well to recall the origin of the concept in the revulsion against Nazism. They would do well to remember the victims of genocide in Cambodia and Rwanda. They would do well to remember Lal Jamilla Mandokhel. It is reasonable and salutary to subject the concept of human rights to philosophical and practical criticism. The contemporary appeal and influence of the concept provide reasons to subject it to critical scrutiny. In this book I have tried to show both the moral power of the concept and the difficult theoretical and practical problems that it raises.

We cannot know the future of human rights, but the social sciences can throw some light on the darkness ahead. Risse and his colleagues, for example, have argued that human-rights advances are brought about by a combination of external and internal pressures on rights-violating states (Risse, Ropp and Sikkink 1999). The Vienna conference of 1993 reinforced the commitment of the international community in principle to universal human rights. Most governments are formally committed to human rights, and the number and effectiveness of human-rights NGOs have greatly increased in recent years. Unashamed human-rights violating states are now much rarer than they were twenty years ago. Yet serious violations continue, especially against vulnerable groups such as women, children, indigenous peoples, minorities, migrant workers and asylum seekers. Here the limits of law and the need for social science are clear. The discourse of human rights has, for example, not taken capitalism seriously. We need a political economy of human rights.

The socialist critique of capitalism has been replaced by a more diffuse concern with 'globalization'. Globalization is a complex and disputed phenomenon (Krasner 2001) that has complex implications for human rights. On the one hand, the concept of human rights is both theoretically *universal* and practically *globalized*. Human-rights activists should be cautious in criticizing globalization, for they are promoting it. On the other hand, the most powerful forces of globalization are states and large, private economic organizations (MNCs), together with the international financial institutions. We have seen that human-rights activists can penetrate this power system, but only with difficulty and with limited results (Fox 2000). Donnelly emphasizes the persistence of state sovereignty as a barrier to human-rights advance (Donnelly 1998:

152–3). This is true, but it is not the whole truth in at least two important respects. The first is that states are not the only abusers of human rights: MNCs and IFIs that are partly independent of states can be human-rights violators. The second is that states do what certain human agents decide that they should do, and the relation between sovereignty and human rights can be changed in the future, as it has been changed in the past.

Problems of intervention

State sovereignty obstructs the implementation of human rights, partly because state leaders have an interest in suppressing human rights, and partly because ordinary people have a limited willingness to make sacrifices to defend the human rights of others. However, even if we can summon the will to defend human rights, it may be very difficult to do so. The NATO intervention in Yugoslavia of 1999 showed this dramatically (Booth 2000; Dunér 2001). The government of Yugoslavia had committed serious human-rights violations against the Albanian people of Kosovo for many years (Amnesty International 1998). This had provoked armed Albanian resistance. The Yugoslav government had responded with brutal repression, involving more, and more serious, human-rights violations. There were fears of ethnic cleansing or even genocide, based in part on memories of recent mass atrocities in other parts of the former Yugoslavia, especially Bosnia. After failed negotiations, NATO bombed Yugoslavia, prompting the very ethnic cleansing it was supposed to avert, and killing large numbers of Yugoslav civilians, as well as inflicting massive economic damage – all this probably in violation of international law, since the Security Council had not called for the action. The Yugoslav government of Slobodan Milosevic was defeated; the Albanians returned home; Milosevic was overthrown and arrested as an indicted international criminal; Yugoslavia became a democracy, while Kosovo is neither stable nor a human-rights utopia. The NATO action probably contributed to the destabilization of neighbouring Macedonia, whose future is currently fragile.

The concept of human rights is hardly adequate to understand this political complexity. It helps to identify the problem, but says rather little about the solution. The legalism of the modern human-rights concept is not up to the task. It may help to say that Iraq's invasion of Kuwait in 1991 was illegal, and that the Iraqi government is a gross violator of human rights, but this may leave us morally uncertain when we hear that economic sanctions against Iraq may be responsible (this is disputed) for the deaths of many thousands of Iraqi children. Even if those intervening from outside are able to stop human-rights violations in the short term, the problems of creating the economic, social and political conditions for just and stable reconstruction are formidable.

The dilemma of human-rights intervention is that not intervening seems to mock the idealistic declarations of human rights, while interventions may be enormously costly and may even be counter-productive. This explains the actual, tentative responses of the international community to human-rights disasters, such as Rwanda, Bosnia and Kosovo: its human-rights commitments mean that it doesn't want to do nothing, while the principle of limited sacrifice means that it doesn't want to do much. Thus, it usually does too little too late. After humanitarian and human-rights disasters such as Kosovo, the 'international community', and especially the governments of the rich and powerful states, are typically quick and generous in 'pledging' assistance for social reconstruction but slower and less generous in delivering it (Patrick 2000).

There is much talk in academic and political circles about the need for 'early warning' of human-rights disasters. This raises another difficult problem. We now have fairly good social-scientific knowledge about the early-warning signs of human-rights disasters. Relatively small-scale but persistent and systematic human-rights violations are often the precursors of much greater ones. The Nazi genocide of the Jews was preceded by several years of *relatively* minor human-rights violations, such as discrimination in employment (Schleunes 1970). Although effective human-rights pressure from governments and NGOs and skilful conflict-resolution diplomacy may both improve the human-rights situation and reduce the risk of disaster (Gurr 2000), this may leave a difficult question of *when* to intervene. There were early warnings of disaster in Kosovo in the 1980s and a new set in the early 1990s. The problem is that the concept of early warning suggests early intervention, but early intervention may easily be disproportionate and counter-productive. The international human-rights movement may help to prevent human-rights violations from becoming human-rights catastrophes, but the concept of early warning does not resolve all the dilemmas of intervention.

Concluding remarks

Since the end of the cold war, Western policy-makers have presented human rights, democracy and market economies as a package. The relations between markets and human rights are, however, complex, problematic and not well understood. The relations between democracy and human rights are also problematic, because, although democracies generally respect human rights better than authoritarian regimes do, democracies can violate human rights, and the protection of human rights may require limitations on democracy. In practice, the Western powers have interpreted 'democracy' to mean free and fair elections, and, desirable though these are, they are not only not sufficient conditions for the protection of human rights, but sometimes accompany, and perhaps even cause, the deterioration of human rights. In many recent cases, this has been because elected governments have pursued market-based economic policies that have not only worsened the protection of economic and social rights for the most vulnerable sections of society (especially women), but also provoked increases in crime that have led to restrictions on civil and political rights (Panizza 1995). We must also distinguish between *democracy* and *democratization*, the process of political change that has a problematic relation to human rights for somewhat different reasons. The transition from authoritarianism to democracy may be a change from imposed order to regulated conflict. Where there is little or no tradition of democratic politics, and also economic hardship and/or ethnic divisions, the restraints that democracy places on conflict may break down. The results may resemble the human-rights catastrophes of Rwanda or Yugoslavia, in both of which countries the processes of democratization were involved in the ensuing human-rights tragedies.

The twenty-first century begins with the future of human rights uncertain. Great advances have been made since 1945, not only in standard-setting (international and national laws) and institution-building (human-rights commissions, committees, courts, etc.), but also in freedom and well-being for many people in many countries. There are still many countries in which civil and political rights are trampled on. Progress towards the recognition of economic and social rights has been slow and largely rhetorical. Worse, the fashion for neo-liberal economic policies has reduced the protection of these rights for millions of people around the world who enjoy them least. There is a tendency among human-rights academics to devote excessive attention to the UN system of commissions and committees. These may be important, but they are certainly not the only important institutions that affect human rights in the world, and they are probably not the most important. The concept of human rights is centrally concerned with the misuse of *power*. The social-scientific study of human rights should give priority to the primary centres of power and to the possible sources of resistance. This entails that human-rights studies should attend more to the G7, the Bretton Woods institutions, and the foreign policy of the USA. The study of human rights should be integrated with political economy, development economics, conflict studies and the politics of democratic transition. The political theory of human rights has, since Locke, accorded to the rule of law a central place in the protection of human rights. This is correct. Nevertheless, both the theory and practice of human rights have suffered from being excessively legalistic. The kind of economics practised by Amartya Sen and the kind of applied moral philosophy developed by Martha Nussbaum may have more to contribute to the advance of human-rights knowledge than refined legal analysis of human-rights texts (Sen 1981; 2001; Drèze and Sen 1990–1; Nussbaum and Sen 1993).

Donnelly has said that the struggle for human rights will be won or lost at the national level (Donnelly 1994: 117).

This is only a partial truth. It is true that, notwithstanding globalization, the nation-state is still an important field of power. It is also true that, for many people, the single most important power that affects their human rights is their state and its institutions, especially its legal and law-enforcement agencies. It is also true, however, that, for many others, the structures and processes of the global economy and of global politics are more important. We should recall that many private corporations are richer and more powerful than many states. Risse and his colleagues rightly argue that a complex and finely judged mix of states and NGOs, of internal and external actors, provide the best hope for human rights in the coming years. We have seen that human-rights NGOs have increased greatly in number in recent years, not least in poor countries. Important distinctions are emerging between *international* NGOs, *national* NGOs and *grass-roots* or *community-based* NGOs. Observers have noted tensions among these different types of NGO, especially between those from the rich North and the poor South. I have suggested that these tensions may be healthy because they entail *the democratization of the human-rights movement*, that is, the bridging of the gap between the discourse and practices of UN diplomats and human-rights lawyers and the ordinary people of the world, to protect whose dignity, freedom and well-being the Universal Declaration of Human Rights was adopted (Morsink 1999a). Anthropology may have a special contribution to make to understanding this aspect of human rights, for it can link the concept of human rights to the cultural understandings of real people in real situations (Wilson 1997c). In addition, a kind of applied human-rights anthropology is being carried out by various projects of human-rights education, both formal and informal, around the world (Andreopoulos and Claude 1997). The social sciences have, after too long a delay, begun to take human rights seriously. We should hope that this welcome development will be accompanied by human-rights activists taking social science seriously.

References

Aidoo, A. 1993: Africa: democracy without human rights? *Human Rights Quarterly*, 15 (4), 703–15.

Alston, P. 1992a: The Commission on Human Rights. In P. Alston (ed.), *The United Nations and Human Rights: a critical appraisal.* Oxford: Clarendon Press, 126–210.

Alston, P. 1992b: The Committee on Economic, Social and Cultural Rights. In P. Alston (ed.), *The United Nations and Human Rights: a critical appraisal.* Oxford: Clarendon Press, 473–508.

Alston, P. 1994: The UN's human rights record: from San Francisco to Vienna and beyond. *Human Rights Quarterly*, 16 (2), 375–90.

American Anthropological Association Executive Board 1947: Statement on human rights submitted to the Commission on Human Rights, United Nations. *American Anthropologist*, new series, 49 (4), 539–43.

Amnesty International 1993: *Getting Away With Murder: political killings and 'disappearances' in the 1990s.* London: Amnesty International Publications.

Amnesty International 1998: *Kosovo: the evidence.* London: Amnesty International United Kingdom.

Amnesty International 1999: *Amnesty International Children's Action 1999 – Report.* ⟨http://www.amnesty.org/ailib/intcam/children/kids99/kidappe.htm⟩.

Andreassen, B.-A., Skålnes, T., Smith, A. G. and Stokke, H. 1988: Assessing human rights performance in developing countries: the case for a minimal threshold approach to the economic and social rights. In B.-A. Andreassen and A. Eide (eds), *Human Rights in Developing Countries 1987/88.* Copenhagen: Akademisk Ferlag, 333–55.

Andreopoulos, G. J. and Claude, R. P. (eds) 1997: *Human Rights Education for the Twenty-First Century*. Philadelphia: University of Pennsylvania Press.

An-Na'im, A. A. 1992: Toward a cross-cultural approach to defining international standards of human rights: the meaning of cruel, inhuman, or degrading treatment or punishment. In A. A. An-Na'im (ed.), *Human Rights in Cross-Cultural Perspectives: a quest for consensus*. Philadelphia: University of Pennsylvania Press, 19–43.

Arai, Y. 1998: The margin of appreciation doctrine in the jurisprudence of Article 8 of the European Convention on Human Rights. *Netherlands Quarterly of Human* Rights, 16 (1), 41–61.

Arat, Z. F. 1991: *Democracy and Human Rights in Developing Countries*. Boulder, CO: Lynne Rienner.

Ashcraft, R. 1986: *Revolutionary Politics and Locke's Two Treatises of Government*. Princeton, NJ: Princeton University Press.

Ashworth, G. 1999: The silencing of women. In T. Dunne and N. J. Wheeler (eds), *Human Rights in Global Politics*. Cambridge: Cambridge University Press, 259–76.

Baehr, P. R. 1996: *The Role of Human Rights in Foreign Policy*. 2nd edn, Basingstoke: Macmillan.

Baehr, P. R. 1999: *Human Rights: universality in practice*. Basingstoke: Macmillan.

Bailyn, B. 1992: *The Ideological Origins of the American Revolution*. Enlarged edn, Cambridge, MA: Harvard University Press.

Baker, K. M. 1994: The idea of a declaration of rights. In D. Van Kley (ed.), *The French Idea of Freedom: the Old Regime and the Declaration of Rights of 1789*. Stanford, CA: Stanford University Press, 154–96.

Barnett, C. R. 1988: Is there a scientific basis in anthropology for the ethics of human rights? In T. E. Downing and G. Kushner (eds), *Human Rights and Anthropology*. Cambridge, MA: Cultural Survival, 21–6.

Barnett, H. G. 1948: On science and human rights. *American Anthropologist*, new series, 50 (2), 352–5.

Barry, B. M. 1965: *Political Argument*. London: Routledge & Kegan Paul.

Barry, B. M. 2000: Is there a right to development? In T. Coates (ed.), *International Justice*. Aldershot: Ashgate, 9–23.

Barry, B. M. 2001: *Culture and Equality: an egalitarian critique of multiculturalism*. Cambridge: Polity.

Becker, C. 1966: *The Declaration of Independence: a study in the history of political ideas*. New York: Alfred A. Knopf.

Beitz, C. 1979: Human rights and social justice. In P. G. Brown and D. MacLean (eds), *Human Rights and U. S. Foreign Policy*. Lexington, MA: Lexington Books, 45–63.

Bell, D. A., Brown, D., Jayasuriya, K. and Jones, D. M. 1995: *Towards Illiberal Democracy in Pacific Asia*. New York: St Martin's Press.

Bellah, R. N. 1983: The ethical aims of social inquiry. In N. Haan, R. N. Bellah, P. Rabinow and W. M. Sullivan (eds), *Social Science as Moral Inquiry*. New York: Columbia University Press, 360–81.

Bellah, R. N., Haan, N., Rabinow, P. and Sullivan, W. M. 1983: Introduction. In N. Haan, R. N. Bellah, P. Rabinow and W. M. Sullivan (eds), *Social Science as Moral Inquiry*. New York: Columbia University Press, 1–18.

Beran, H. 1984: A liberal theory of secession. *Political Studies*, 32 (1), 21–31.

Beran, H. 1988: More theory of secession: a response to Birch. *Political Studies*, 36 (2), 316–23.

Bielefeldt, H. 2000: 'Western' versus 'Islamic' human rights conceptions? A critique of cultural essentialism in the discussion on human rights. *Political Theory*, 28 (1), 90–121.

Binion, G. 1995: Human rights: a feminist perspective. *Human Rights Quarterly*, 17 (3), 509–26.

Birch, A. H. 1984: Another liberal theory of secession. *Political Studies*, 32 (4), 596–602.

Booth, K. (ed.) 2000: *The Kosovo Tragedy: the human rights dimension. International Journal of Human Rights*, 4 (3/4) [special issue].

Bradlow, D. D. and Grossman, C. 1995: Limited mandates and intertwined problems: a new challenge for the World Bank and the IMF. *Human Rights Quarterly*, 17 (3), 411–42.

Brett, R. 1995: The role and limits of human rights NGOs at the United Nations. *Political Studies*, 43, 96–110 [special issue, *Politics and Human Rights*].

Brown, C. 1999: Universal human rights: a critique. In T. Dunne and N. J. Wheeler (eds), *Human Rights in Global Politics*. Cambridge: Cambridge University Press, 103–27.

Byrnes, A. 1992: The Committee against Torture. In P. Alston (ed.), *The United Nations and Human Rights: a critical appraisal*. Oxford: Clarendon Press, 509–46.

Caney, S. 1992: Liberalism and communitarianism: a misconceived debate. *Political Studies*, 40 (2), 273–89.

Carr, E. H. 1949: The Rights of Man. In UNESCO (ed.), *Human Rights: comments and interpretations*. Westport, CT: Greenwood Press, 19–23.

Cassel, D. 1996: Corporate initiatives: a second human rights revolution? *Fordham International Law Journal*, 19, 1963–84.

Cassese, A. 1992: The General Assembly: historical perspective 1945–1989. In P. Alston (ed.), *The United Nations and Human Rights: a critical appraisal*. Oxford: Clarendon Press, 25–54.

Cassese, A. 1995: *Self-Determination of Peoples: a legal reappraisal*. New York: Cambridge University Press.

Chan, J. 1999: A Confucian perspective on human rights for contemporary China. In J. A. Bauer and D. A. Bell (eds), *The East Asian Challenge for Human Rights*. Cambridge: Cambridge University Press, 212–37.

Chaplin, J. 1993: How much cultural and religious pluralism can liberalism tolerate? In J. Horton (ed.), *Multiculturalism and Toleration*. Basingstoke: Macmillan, 39–46.

Christie, K. 1995: Regime security and human rights in Southeast Asia. *Political Studies*, 43, 204–18 [special issue, *Politics and Human Rights*].

Chun, L. 2001: Human rights and democracy: the case for decoupling. *International Journal of Human Rights*, 5 (3), 19–44.

Cingranelli, D. L. and Richards, D. L. 1999: Respect for human rights after the end of the cold war. *Journal of Peace Research*, 36 (5), 511–34.

Clark, A. M. 2001: *Diplomacy of Conscience: Amnesty International and changing human rights norms*. Princeton, NJ: Princeton University Press.

Claude, R. P. 1976: The classical model of human rights development. In R. P. Claude (ed.), *Comparative Human Rights*. Baltimore: Johns Hopkins University Press, 6–50.

Claude, R. P. 2002: Personal communication.

Claude, R. P. and Weston, B. H. 1992: International human rights: overviews. In R. P. Claude and B. H. Weston (eds), *Human Rights in the World Community: issues and action*. 2nd edn, Philadelphia: University of Pennsylvania Press, 1–14.

Cleary, S. 1996: The World Bank and NGOs. In P. Willetts (ed.), *'The Conscience of the World': the influence of non-governmental organisations in the UN system*. Washington, DC: Brookings Institution, 63–97.

Cohen, C. P. 1990: The role of non-governmental organizations in the drafting of the Convention on the Rights of the Child. *Human Rights Quarterly*, 12 (1), 137–47.

Coomaraswamy, R. 1999: Reinventing international law: women's rights as human rights in the international community. In P. Van Ness (ed.), *Debating Human Rights: critical essays from the United States and Asia*. London: Routledge, 167–83.

Cranston, M. 1973: *What are Human Rights?* London: Bodley Head.

Dagger, R. 1989: Rights. In T. Ball, J. Farr and R. L. Hanson (eds), *Political Innovation and Conceptual Change*. Cambridge: Cambridge University Press, 292–308.

Dahl, R. 1989: *Democracy and its Critics*. New Haven, CT: Yale University Press.

Davenport, C. A. 1996: 'Constitutional promises' and repressive reality: a cross-national time-series investigation of why political and civil liberties are suppressed. *Journal of Politics*, 58 (3), 627–54.

Desai, M. 1999: From Vienna to Beijing: women's human rights activism and the human rights community. In P. Van Ness (ed.), *Debating Human Rights: critical essays from the United States and Asia*. London: Routledge, 184–96.

Dickinson, H. T. 1977: *Political Ideology in Eighteenth-Century Britain*. London: Methuen.

Donnelly, J. 1982: Human rights as natural rights. *Human Rights Quarterly*, 4 (3), 391–405.

Donnelly, J. 1985a: *The Concept of Human Rights*. London: Croom Helm.

Donnelly, J. 1985b: In search of the unicorn: the jurisprudence and politics of the right to development. *California Western International Law Journal*, 15 (3), 473–509.

Donnelly, J. 1986: International human rights: a regime analysis. *International Organization*, 40 (3), 599–642.

Donnelly, J. 1989: *Universal Human Rights in Theory and Practice*. Ithaca, NY: Cornell University Press.

Donnelly, J. 1993: Third generation rights. In C. Brölmann, R. Lefeber and M. Zieck (eds), *Peoples and Minorities in International Law*. Dordrecht: Martinus Nijhoff, 119–50.

Donnelly, J. 1994: Post-cold war reflections on the study of international human rights. *Ethics and International Affairs*, 8, 97–117.

Donnelly, J. 1998: *International Human Rights*. 2nd edn, Boulder, CO: Westview Press.

Donnelly, J. 1999: The social construction of international human rights. In T. Dunne and N. J. Wheeler (eds), *Human Rights in Global Politics*. Cambridge: Cambridge University Press, 71–102.

Donnelly, J. 2000: An overview. In D. P. Forsythe (ed.), *Human Rights and Comparative Foreign Policy*. Tokyo: United Nations University Press, 310–34.

Donnelly, J. 2001: The Universal Declaration model of human rights: a liberal defense', *Human Rights Working Papers*, no. 12,

⟨http://www.du.edu/humanrights/workingpapers/papers/12-donnelly-02-01.pdf⟩.

Doughty, P. L. 1988: Crossroads for anthropology: human rights in Latin America. In T. E. Downing and G. Kushner (eds), *Human Rights and Anthropology*. Cambridge, MA: Cultural Survival, 43–71.

Downing, T. E. 1988: Human rights research: the challenge for anthropologists. In T. E. Downing and G. Kushner (eds), *Human Rights and Anthropology*. Cambridge, MA: Cultural Survival, 9–19.

Downing, T. E. and Kushner, G. 1988: Introduction. In T. E. Downing and G. Kushner (eds), *Human Rights and Anthropology*. Cambridge, MA: Cultural Survival, 1–8.

Drèze, J. and Sen, A. (eds) 1990–1: *The Political Economy of Hunger*. Oxford: Clarendon Press.

Dunér, B. 2001: Violence for human rights. *International Journal of Human Rights*, 5 (2), 46–71.

Dunne, T. and Wheeler, N. J. (eds) 1999: *Human Rights in Global Politics*. Cambridge: Cambridge University Press.

Dworkin, R. 1978: *Taking Rights Seriously*. London: Duckworth.

Dworkin, R. 1996: *Freedom's Law: the moral reading of the American constitution*. Cambridge, MA: Harvard University Press.

Edwards, M. and Hulme, D. 1996: Introduction: NGO performance and accountability. In M. Edwards and D. Hulme (eds), *Beyond the Magic Bullet: NGO performance and accountability in the post-cold war world*. West Hartford, CT: Kumarian Press, 1–19.

Eide, A. 1989: Realization of social and economic rights and the minimum threshold approach. *Human Rights Law Journal*, 10 (1–2), 35–51.

Eide, A. 1992: The Sub-Commission on Prevention of Discrimination and Protection of Minorities. In P. Alston (ed.), *The United Nations and Human Rights: a critical appraisal*. Oxford: Clarendon Press, 211–64.

Eide, A. 1993: In search of constructive alternatives to secession. In C. Tomuschat (ed.), *Modern Law of Self-determination*. Dordrecht: Martinus Nijhoff, 139–76.

Espiell, H. G. 1981: The right of development as a human right. *Texas International Law Journal*, 16 (2), 189–205.

Evans, T. 1998: Introduction: power, hegemony and the universalization of human rights. In T. Evans (ed.), *Human Rights Fifty Years On: a reappraisal*. Manchester: Manchester University Press, 2–23.

Evans, T. 2001: *The Politics of Human Rights*. London: Pluto Press.

Falk, R. 1992: Cultural foundations for the international protection of human rights. In A. A. An-Na'im (ed.), *Human Rights in Cross-Cultural Perspectives: a quest for consensus*. Philadelphia: University of Pennsylvania Press, 44–64.

Fein, H. 1995: More murder in the middle: life-integrity violations and democracy in the world, 1987. *Human Rights Quarterly*, 17 (1), 170–91.

Fellmeth, A. X. 2000: Feminism and international law: theory, methodology, and substantive reform. *Human Rights Quarterly*, 22 (3), 658–733.

Forsythe, D. P. 1989: *Human Rights and World Politics*. 2nd edn, Lincoln: University of Nebraska Press.

Forsythe, D. P. 1995: The UN and human rights at fifty: an incremental but incomplete revolution. *Global Governance*, 1, 297–318.

Forsythe, D. P. 1997: The United Nations, human rights, and development. *Human Rights Quarterly*, 19 (2), 334–49.

Forsythe, D. P. 2000: *Human Rights in International Relations*. Cambridge: Cambridge University Press.

Foweraker, J. and Landman, T. 1997: *Citizenship Rights and Social Movements: a comparative and statistical analysis*. Oxford: Oxford University Press.

Fox, J. A. 2000: The World Bank Inspection Panel: lessons from the first five years. *Global Governance*, 6 (3), 279–318.

Freeman, M. A. 1980: *Edmund Burke and the Critique of Political Radicalism*. Oxford: Basil Blackwell.

Freeman, M. A. 1999: Fifty years of development of the concept and contents of human rights. In P. Baehr, C. Flinterman and M. Senders (eds), *Innovation and Inspiration: fifty years of the Universal Declaration of Human Rights*. Amsterdam: Royal Netherlands Academy of Arts and Sciences, 27–47.

Gandhi, M. 1949: A letter addressed to the Director-General of UNESCO. In UNESCO (ed.), *Human Rights: comments and interpretations*. Westport, CT: Greenwood Press, 18.

Gewirth, A. 1978: *Reason and Morality*. Chicago: University of Chicago Press.

Gewirth, A. 1981: The basis and content of human rights. In J. R. Pennock and J. W. Chapman (eds), *Human Rights*. New York: New York University Press, 121–47.

Gewirth, A. 1982: *Human Rights: essays on justification and applications*. Chicago: University of Chicago Press.

Gewirth, A. 1996: *The Community of Rights*. Chicago: University of Chicago Press.

Glover, J. 1999: *Humanity: a moral history of the twentieth century*. London: Jonathan Cape.

Goodin, R. E. 1979: The development-rights trade-off: some unwarranted economic and political assumptions. *Universal Human Rights*, 1 (2), 31–42.

Gray, J. 1986: *Liberalism*. Milton Keynes: Open University Press.

Gross, O. and Aoláin, F. N. 2001: From discretion to scrutiny: revisiting the application of the margin of appreciation doctrine in the context of Article 15 of the European Convention on Human Rights. *Human Rights Quarterly*, 23 (3), 625–49.

Gurr, T. R. 1986: The political origins of state violence and terror: a theoretical analysis. In M. Stohl and G. A. Lopez (eds), *Government Violence and Repression: an agenda for research*. New York: Greenwood Press, 45–71.

Gurr, T. R. 2000: *Peoples versus States: minorities at risk in the new century*. Washington, DC: United States Institute of Peace Press.

Gutman, A. (ed.) 1994: *Multiculturalism: examining the politics of recognition*. Princeton, NJ: Princeton University Press.

Hallie, P. 1979: *Lest Innocent Blood Be Shed: the story of the village of Le Chambon and how goodness happened there*. New York: Harper Torchbooks.

Hannum, H. 1990: *Autonomy, Sovereignty and Self-Determination: the accommodation of conflicting rights*. Philadelphia: University of Pennsylvania Press.

Hart, H. L. A. 1982: *Essays on Bentham: studies in jurisprudence and political theory*. Oxford: Clarendon Press.

Held, D., McGrew, A., Goldblatt, D. and Perraton, J. 1999: *Global Transformations: politics, economics and culture*. Cambridge: Polity.

Henderson, C. W. 1991: Conditions affecting the use of political repression. *Journal of Conflict Resolution*, 35 (1), 120–42.

Hirschman, A. O. 1983: Morality and the social sciences: a durable tension. In N. Haan, R. N. Bellah, P. Rabinow and W. M. Sullivan (eds), *Social Science as Moral Inquiry*. New York: Columbia University Press, 21–32.

Hitchcock, D. I. 1994: *Asian Values and the United States: how much conflict?* Washington, DC: Center for Strategic and International Studies.

Holmes, S. T. 1979: Aristippus in and out of Athens. *American Political Science Review*, 73 (1), 113–28.

Holt, J. C. 1965: *Magna Carta*. Cambridge: Cambridge University Press.

Howard, R. E. 1986: *Human Rights in Commonwealth Africa*. Totowa, NJ: Rowman & Littlefield.

Howard, R. E. 1995: *Human Rights and the Search for Community*. Boulder, CO: Westview Press.

Hunt, L. (ed.) 1996: *The French Revolution and Human Rights: a brief documentary history*. Boston: St Martin's Press.

Hunt, P. 1996: *Reclaiming Social Rights: international and comparative perspectives*. Aldershot: Ashgate.

International Criminal Tribunal for the Former Yugoslavia 2001: *Indictments and Proceedings: the prosecutor of the tribunal against Slobodan Milosevic and others*. ⟨http://www.un.org./icty/indictment/english/mil-ai010629e.htm⟩.

Jacobson, R. 1992: The Committee on the Elimination of Discrimination against Women. In P. Alston (ed.), *The United Nations and Human Rights: a critical appraisal*. Oxford: Clarendon Press, 444–72.

Jones, P. 1994: *Rights*. Basingstoke: Macmillan.

Keck, M. E. and Sikkink, K. 1998: *Activists Beyond Borders: advocacy networks in international politics*. Ithaca, NY: Cornell University Press.

Kingsbury, B. 1999: The applicability of the international legal concept of 'indigenous peoples' in Asia. In J. R. Bauer and D. A. Bell (eds), *The East Asian Challenge for Human Rights*. Cambridge: Cambridge University Press, 336–77.

Korey, W. 1998: *NGOs and the Universal Declaration of Human Rights: 'a curious grapevine'*. Basingstoke: Macmillan.

Krasner, S. D. 1995: Sovereignty, regimes, and human rights. In V. Rittberger and P. Mayer (eds), *Regime Theory and International Relations*. Oxford: Clarendon Press, 139–67.

Krasner, S. D. 2001: Abiding sovereignty. *International Political Science Review*, 22 (3), 229–51.

Kymlicka, W. 1989: *Liberalism, Community and Culture*. Oxford: Clarendon Press.

Kymlicka, W. 1990: *Contemporary Political Philosophy: an introduction*. Oxford: Clarendon Press.

Kymlicka, W. 1995: *Multicultural Citizenship: a liberal theory of group rights*. Oxford: Clarendon Press.

Kymlicka, W. 2001: Human rights and ethnocultural justice. In W. Kymlicka, *Politics in the Vernacular: nationalism, multiculturalism and citizenship*. Oxford: Oxford University Press, 69–90.

Leary, V. A. 1992: Lessons from the experience of the International Labour Organization. In P. Alston (ed.), *The United Nations and Human Rights: a critical appraisal*. Oxford: Clarendon Press, 580–619.

Locke, J. [1689] 1970: *Two Treatises of Government*. Cambridge: Cambridge University Press.

McCamant, J. F. 1981: Social science and human rights. *International Organization*, 35 (3), 531–52.

McCorquodale, R. and Fairbrother, R. 1999: Globalization and human rights. *Human Rights Quarterly*, 21 (3), 735–66.

Macdonald, M. 1963: Natural rights. In P. Laslett (ed.), *Philosophy, Politics and Society*. Oxford: Basil Blackwell, 35–55.

McGarry, J. and O'Leary, B. (eds) 1993: *The Politics of Ethnic Conflict Regulation*. London: Routledge.

McGrew, A. G. 1998: Human rights in a global age: coming to terms with globalization. In T. Evans (ed.), *Human Rights Fifty Years On: a reappraisal*. Manchester: Manchester University Press, 188–210.

MacIntyre, A. 1981: *After Virtue*. Notre Dame, IN: University of Notre Dame Press.

McNally, D. 1989: Locke, Levellers and liberty: property and democracy in the thought of the first Whigs. *History of Political Thought*, 10 (1), 17–40.

Macpherson, C. B. 1962: *The Political Theory of Possessive Individualism*. Oxford: Clarendon Press.

Margalit, A. and Raz, J. 1990: National self-determination. *Journal of Philosophy*, 87 (9), 439–61.

Maritain, J. 1949: Introduction. In UNESCO (ed.), *Human Rights: comments and interpretations*. Westport, CT: Greenwood Press, 9–17.

Messer, E. 1993: Anthropology and human rights. *Annual Review of Anthropology*, 22, 221–49.

Meyer, W. H. 1996: Human rights and MNCs: theory versus quantitative analysis. *Human Rights Quarterly*, 18 (2), 368–97.

Meyer, W. H. 1998: *Human Rights and International Political Economy in Third World Nations*. Westport, CT: Praeger.

Meyer, W. H. 1999: Confirming, infirming, and 'falsifying' theories of human rights: reflections on Smith, Bolyard, and Ippolito through the lens of Lakatos. *Human Rights Quarterly*, 21 (1), 220–8.

Milgram, S. 1974: *Obedience to Authority: an experimental view*. New York: Harper & Row.

Miller, D. 1995: *On Nationality*. Oxford: Clarendon Press.

Miller, F. Jr 1995: *Nature, Justice, and Rights in Aristotle's Politics*. Oxford: Clarendon Press.

Milner, W. T., Poe, S. C. and Leblang, D. 1999: Security rights, subsistence rights and liberties: a theoretical survey of the empirical landscape. *Human Rights Quarterly*, 21 (2), 403–43.

Mitchell, N. J. and McCormick, J. M. 1988: Economic and political explanations of human rights violations. *World Politics*, 40 (4), 476–98.

Moon, B. E. 1991: *The Political Economy of Basic Human Needs*. Ithaca, NY: Cornell University Press.

Morsink, J. 1999a: *The Universal Declaration of Human Rights: origins, drafting, and intent.* Philadelphia: University of Pennsylvania Press.

Morsink, J. 1999b: Cultural genocide, the Universal Declaration, and minority rights. *Human Rights Quarterly,* 21 (4), 1009–60.

Mulhall, S. and Swift, A. 1996: *Liberals and Communitarians.* 2nd edn, Oxford: Basil Blackwell.

Nickel, J. W. 1987: *Making Sense of Human Rights: philosophical reflections on the Universal Declaration of Human Rights.* Berkeley: University of California Press.

Nussbaum, M. C. 1992: Human functioning and social justice: in defence of Aristotelian essentialism. *Political Theory,* 20 (2), 202–46.

Nussbaum, M. C. 1993: Commentary on Onora O'Neill: justice, gender, and international boundaries. In M. Nussbaum and A. Sen (eds), *The Quality of Life.* Oxford: Clarendon Press, 324–35.

Nussbaum, M. C. 2000: *Women and Human Development: the capabilities approach.* Cambridge: Cambridge University Press.

Nussbaum, M. C. and Sen, A. (eds) 1993: *The Quality of Life.* Oxford: Clarendon Press.

O'Donovan, D. 1992: The Economic and Social Council. In P. Alston (ed.), *The United Nations and Human Rights: a critical appraisal.* Oxford: Clarendon Press, 107–25.

Office of the United Nations High Commissioner for Human Rights 2001: *Status of Ratification of the Principal International Human Rights Treaties.* ⟨http://www.unhchr.ch/pdf/report.pdf⟩.

Oliner, S. P. and Oliner, P. M. 1988: *The Altruistic Personality: rescuers of Jews in Nazi Europe.* New York: Free Press.

Oloka-Onyango, J. and Udagama, D. 2000: *The Realization of Economic, Social and Cultural Rights: globalization and its impact on the full enjoyment of human rights.* Preliminary report submitted to the UN Sub-Commission on the Promotion and Protection of Human Rights, 52nd session, 15 June, E/CN.4/Sub.2/2000/13.

O'Neill, O. 1993: Justice, gender, and international boundaries. In M. Nussbaum and A. Sen (eds), *The Quality of Life.* Oxford: Clarendon Press, 303–23.

Opsahl, T. 1992: The Human Rights Committee. In P. Alston (ed.), *The United Nations and Human Rights: a critical appraisal.* Oxford: Clarendon Press, 369–443.

Osborn, A. 2001: Milosevic to face genocide charge. *The Guardian,* 31 August, 2.

Othman, N. 1999: Grounding human rights arguments in non-Western culture: *Shari'a* and the citizenship rights of women in a modern Islamic state. In J. A. Bauer and D. A. Bell (eds), *The*

East Asian Challenge for Human Rights. Cambridge: Cambridge University Press, 169–92.

Otto, D. 1996: Non-governmental organizations in the United Nations system: the emerging role of international civil society. *Human Rights Quarterly*, 18 (1), 107–41.

Paine, T. [1791–2] 1988: *The Rights of Man*. Harmondsworth: Penguin Books.

Panizza, F. 1995: Human rights in the processes of transition and consolidation of democracy in Latin America. *Political Studies*, 43, 168–88 [special issue, *Politics and Human Rights*].

Parekh, B. 1994: Decolonizing liberalism. In A. Shtromas (ed.), *The End of Isms? Reflections on the fate of ideological politics after communism's collapse*. Oxford: Basil Blackwell, 85–103.

Parekh, B. 1999: Non-ethnocentric universalism. In T. Dunne and N. J. Wheeler (eds), *Human Rights in Global Politics*. Cambridge: Cambridge University Press, 128–59.

Patrick, S. 2000: The check is in the mail: improving the delivery and coordination of postconflict assistance. *Global Governance*, 6 (1), 61–94.

Peterson, V. S. and Parisi, L. 1998: Are women human? It's not an academic question. In T. Evans (ed.), *Human Rights Fifty Years On: a reappraisal*. Manchester: Manchester University Press, 132–60.

Philp, M. 1989: *Paine*. Oxford: Oxford University Press.

Poe, S. C. and Tate, C. N. 1994: Repression of human rights to personal integrity in the 1980s: a global analysis. *American Political Science Review*, 88 (4), 853–72.

Preis, A-B. S. 1996: Human rights as cultural practice: an anthropological critique. *Human Rights Quarterly*, 18 (2), 286–315.

Pritchard, K. 1989: Political science and the teaching of human rights. *Human Rights Quarterly*, 11 (3), 459–75.

Rawls, J. 1993: The law of peoples. In S. Shute and S. Hurley (eds), *On Human Rights: the Oxford Amnesty lectures 1993*. New York: Basic Books, 41–82.

Rawls, J. 1999: *The Law of Peoples*. Cambridge, MA: Harvard University Press.

Raz, J. 1986: *The Morality of Freedom*. Oxford: Clarendon Press.

Reanda, L. 1992: The Commission on the Status of Women. In P. Alston (ed.), *The United Nations and Human Rights: a critical appraisal*. Oxford: Clarendon Press, 265–303.

Rich, R. 1988: The right to development: a right of peoples? In J. Crawford (ed.), *The Rights of Peoples*. Oxford: Clarendon Press, 39–54.

Risse, T. and Ropp, S. C. 1999. International human rights norms and domestic change: conclusion. In T. Risse, S. C. Ropp and K.

Sikkink (eds), *The Power of Human Rights: international norms and domestic change*. Cambridge: Cambridge University Press, 234–78.

Risse, T. and Sikkink, K. 1999: The socialization of international human rights norms into domestic practices: introduction. In T. Risse, S. C. Ropp and K. Sikkink (eds), *The Power of Human Rights: international norms and domestic change*. Cambridge: Cambridge University Press, 1–38.

Risse, T., Ropp S. C. and Sikkink, K. (eds) 1999: *The Power of Human Rights: international norms and domestic change*. Cambridge: Cambridge University Press.

Robertson, A. H. and Merrills, J. G. 1996: *Human Rights in the World: an introduction to the study of the international protection of human rights*. Manchester: Manchester University Press.

Rodman, K. A. 1998: 'Think globally, punish locally': nonstate actors, multinational corporations, and human rights sanctions. *Ethics and International Affairs*, 12, 19–41.

Rorty, R. 1993: Human rights, rationality, and sentimentality. In S. Shute and S. Hurley (eds), *On Human Rights: the Oxford Amnesty lectures 1993*. New York: Basic Books, 111–34.

Roshwald, R. 1959: The concept of human rights. *Philosophy and Phenomenological Research*, 19, 354–79.

Rousseau, J.-J. [1762] 1968: *The Social Contract*. Harmondsworth: Penguin Books.

Rummel, R. J. 1994: *Death by Government*. New Brunswick, NJ: Transaction Publishers.

Samson, K. T. 1992: Human rights co-ordination within the UN system. In P. Alston (ed.), *The United Nations and Human Rights: a critical appraisal*. Oxford: Clarendon Press, 620–75.

Schirmer, J. 1988: The dilemma of cultural diversity and equivalency in universal human rights standards. In T. E. Downing and G. Kushner (eds), *Human Rights and Anthropology*. Cambridge, MA: Cultural Survival, 91–106.

Schirmer, J. 1997: Universal and sustainable human rights? Special tribunals in Guatemala. In R. A. Wilson (ed.), *Human Rights, Culture and Context: anthropological perspectives*. London: Pluto Press, 161–86.

Schleunes, K. A. 1970: *The Twisted Road to Auschwitz: Nazi policy toward German Jews 1933–1939*. Urbana: University of Illinois Press.

Schwab, P. and Pollis, A. 2000: Globalization's impact on human rights. In A. Pollis and P. Schwab (eds), *Human Rights: new perspectives, new realities*. Boulder, CO: Lynne Rienner, 209–23.

Sen, A. 1981: *Poverty and Famines: an essay on entitlement and deprivation*. Oxford: Clarendon Press.

Sen, A. 1999: Human rights and economic achievements. In J. R. Bauer and D. A. Bell (eds), *The East Asian Challenge for Human Rights*. Cambridge: Cambridge University Press, 88–99.

Sen, A. 2001: *Development as Freedom*. Oxford: Oxford University Press.

Shehadi, K. S. 1993: *Ethnic Self-Determination and the Break-Up of States*. London: Brassey's.

Shue, H. 1996: *Basic Rights: subsistence, affluence, and U.S. foreign policy*. 2nd edn, Princeton, NJ: Princeton University Press.

Smith, J., Bolyard, M. and Ippolito, A. 1999: Human rights and the global economy: a response to Meyer. *Human Rights Quarterly*, 21 (1), 207–19.

Smith, J., Pagnucco, T. and Lopez, G. A. 1998: Globalizing human rights: the work of transnational human rights NGOs in the 1990s. *Human Rights Quarterly*, 20 (2), 379–412.

Spiro, M. E. 1986: Cultural relativism and the future of anthropology. *Cultural Anthropology*, 1 (3), 259–86.

Stammers, N. 1999: Social movements and the social construction of human rights. *Human Rights Quarterly*, 21 (4), 980–1008.

Steiner, H. 1994: *An Essay on Rights*. Oxford: Basil Blackwell.

Steward, J. H. 1948: Comment on the statement on human rights. *American Anthropologist*, new series, 50 (2), 351–2.

Stoll, D. 1997: To whom should we listen? Human rights activism in two Guatemalan land disputes. In R. A. Wilson (ed.), *Human Rights, Culture and Context: anthropological perspectives*. London: Pluto Press, 187–215.

Strouse, J. C. and Claude, R. P. 1976: Empirical comparative rights research: some preliminary tests of development hypotheses. In R. P. Claude (ed.), *Comparative Human Rights*. Baltimore: Johns Hopkins University Press, 51–67.

Tamir, Y. 1993: *Liberal Nationalism*. Princeton, NJ: Princeton University Press.

Tang, J. T. H. 1995: Human rights in the Asia-Pacific region: competing perspectives, international discord, and the way ahead. In J. T. H. Tang (ed.), *Human Rights and International Relations in the Asia Pacific*. London: Pinter, 1–9.

Taylor, C. 1997: Nationalism and modernity. In R. McKim and J. McMahan (eds), *The Morality of Nationalism*. New York: Oxford University Press, 31–55.

Tec, N. 1986: *When Light Pierced the Darkness: Christian rescue of Jews in Nazi-occupied Poland*. New York: Oxford University Press.

Thomas, C. 1998: International financial institutions and social and economic human rights: an exploration. In T. Evans (ed.), *Human*

Rights Fifty Years On: a reappraisal. Manchester: Manchester University Press, 161–85.

Thornberry, P. 1991: *International Law and the Rights of Minorities*. Oxford: Clarendon Press.

Tierney, B. 1988: Villey, Ockham and the origin of individual rights. In J. Witte, Jr and F. S. Alexander (eds), *The Weightier Matters of Law: essays on law and religion: a tribute to Harold J. Berman*. Studies in Religion 51 [Atlanta, GA], 1–31.

Tierney, B. 1989: Origins of natural rights language: texts and contexts, 1150–1250. *History of Political Thought*, 10 (4), 615–46.

Tierney, B. 1992: Natural rights in the thirteenth century: a *Quaestio* of Henry of Ghent. *Speculum*, 67 (1), 58–68.

Tierney, B. 1997: *The Idea of Natural Rights*. Atlanta, GA: Scholars Press.

Tuck, R. 1979: *Natural Rights Theories: their origin and development*. Cambridge: Cambridge University Press.

Tully, J. 1995: *Strange Multiplicity: constitutionalism in an age of diversity*. Cambridge: Cambridge University Press.

Turner, B. S. 1993: Outline of a theory of human rights. *Sociology*, 27 (3), 489–512.

Turner, B. S. 1995: Introduction: rights and communities: prolegomenon to a sociology of rights. *Australian and New Zealand Journal of Sociology*, 31 (2), 1–8.

UNESCO (ed.) 1949, repr. 1971: *Human Rights: comments and interpretations*. New York: Columbia University Press/Westport, CT: Greenwood Press.

United Nations 2001: *The Global Compact*. ⟨http://www.unglobalcompact.org/⟩.

United Nations Development Programme 2001: *Human Development Report 2001*. ⟨http://www.undp.org/hdr2001⟩.

Vincent, R. J. 1986: *Human Rights and International Relations*. Cambridge: Cambridge University Press.

Waldron, J. (ed.) 1987: *'Nonsense Upon Stilts': Bentham, Burke and Marx on the Rights of Man*. London: Methuen.

Waldron, J. 1993: A rights-based critique of constitutional rights. *Oxford Journal of Legal Studies*, 13 (1), 18–51.

Walzer, M. 1980: The moral standing of states. *Philosophy and Public Affairs*, 9 (3), 209–29.

Washburn, W. E. 1985: Ethical perspectives in North American ethnology. In J. Helm (ed.), *1984 Proceedings of the American Ethnological Society*. Washington, DC: American Anthropological Association, 50–64.

Washburn, W. E. 1987: Cultural relativism, human rights, and the AAA. *American Anthropologist*, 89 (4), 939–43.

Waters, M. 1996: Human rights and the universalisation of interests: towards a social constructionist approach. *Sociology*, 30 (3), 593–600.

Welch, C. B. 1984: *Liberty and Utility: the French Idéologues and the transformation of liberalism*. New York: Columbia University Press.

Wilson, R. A. 1997a: Human rights, culture and context: an introduction. In R. A. Wilson (ed.), *Human Rights, Culture and Context: anthropological perspectives*. London: Pluto Press, 1–27.

Wilson, R. A. 1997b: Representing human rights violations: social contexts and subjectivities. In R. A. Wilson (ed.), *Human Rights, Culture and Context: anthropological perspectives*. London: Pluto Press, 134–60.

Wilson, R. A. (ed.) 1997c: *Human Rights, Culture and Context: anthropological perspectives*. London: Pluto Press.

Wiseberg, L. S. 1992: Human rights non-governmental organizations. In R. P. Claude and B. H. Weston (eds), *Human Rights in the World Community: issues and action*. 2nd edn, Philadelphia: University of Pennsylvania Press, 372–83.

Woodiwiss, A. 1998: *Globalisation, Human Rights and Labour Law in Pacific Asia*. Cambridge: Cambridge University Press.

Zanger, S. C. 2000: A global analysis of the effect of political regime changes on life integrity violations, 1977–93. *Journal of Peace Research*, 37 (2), 213–33.

Zuckert, M. P. 1989: Bringing philosophy down from the heavens: natural right in the Roman law. *Review of Politics*, 51 (1), 70–85.

Index

absolutism 19, 76, 168–9
abuse of power 15–16, 167
Africa 85–7
America 23
American Anthropological
    Association 76
American Declaration of
    Independence 23, 55
Amnesty International 46, 144,
    147, 159, 170
ancient Greeks 15–16, 167
Andreassen, B.-A. 164
An-Na'im, A. 113
Antigone 16
Anti-Slavery International 142
Arat, Z. 150
Aristotle 16, 60, 167
Asian values 48, 102
asylum 37, 51
autonomy 64–5, 67, 75, 89,
    106, 117

Barnett, C. R. 92–3
Barry, B. 119–20, 152
basic rights 70
Bentham, J. 27–8, 56, 57, 172
Beran, H. 124–5

Bill of Rights 23
boomerang theory 98, 134–7
Bosnia 175
bourgeois rights 22, 29–30,
    168
Brazil 80, 138–9
Bretton Woods 160, 163, 177
Burke, E. 27, 56, 57, 172

capabilities 65–8
capitalism 30, 51, 54, 79, 82,
    85–6, 88–9, 98, 105, 138,
    148–9, 151, 157–9, 163,
    173
Carr, E. H. 58
Carter, Jimmy 46, 78, 94, 170
Cingranelli, D. L. and Richards,
    D. L. 140–1, 157
citizenship rights 16, 74, 83–4,
    167
civil rights 18, 60
civil and political rights 36,
    41, 46, 47, 52, 71, 76,
    80–1, 82–3, 95, 105, 139,
    147, 148, 149–51, 157,
    161, 165, 168, 170, 176,
    177

civil society 26
Claude, R. 79, 138
cold war 9, 43–4, 47, 138,
    140–1, 148, 169, 171
collective rights 117–18,
    120–1, 123, 125, 152–3
colonialism 86, 111, 121–2
Commission on the Status of
    Women 127
Committee on Economic,
    Social and Cultural Rights
    53, 165
common good *see* public
    good
communism 29–30, 149,
    169–70, 171
communitarianism 107,
    125–6
community 18–19, 21, 40, 73,
    75, 103, 105, 107, 117
community-based organizations
    144, 163, 178
compossibility 5, 71
concept of human rights 2,
    5–6
  legal concept 3, 6–7
  political concept 7, 9–10
conceptual analysis 2
Conference on Security and
    Co-operation in Europe
    (CSCE) 47
conflicts of rights 5, 57, 67,
    69–71, 75
conformity 91
consensus 24, 58, 64, 75
constitutionalism 24, 72,
    118–19
Convention on the Elimination
    of Discrimination against
    Women (CEDAW) 46,
    112, 127, 128
Convention on the Elimination
    of Racial Discrimination
    43

corporate codes of conduct
    159
cruelty 90
cultural relativism 27, 42, 48,
    64, 76–7, 83, 86–7, 88,
    92, 93, 97, 99, 102,
    105–14, 129
Cultural Survival 92

Dahl, R. 72
Davenport, C. 157
Declaration on the Elimination
    of Violence Against
    Women 129
Declaration of the Rights of
    Man and the Citizen 24,
    36, 57
Declaration on the Right to
    Development 152
Declaration on the Rights of
    Persons Belonging to
    National or Ethnic,
    Religious and Linguistic
    Minorities 115
decolonization 43
democracy 71–3, 115–16, 125,
    140–1, 150, 151, 176
democratization 81, 140–1,
    157, 170, 176
democratization of human
    rights 146, 178
dialogue 106, 112–13, 118–19,
    138, 163
dignity 65, 71–2, 75, 105–6,
    109, 111, 120, 121
discourse analysis 87
Dominicans 18
Donnelly, J. 15, 22, 42, 62,
    64–5, 68, 70, 71, 74, 75,
    80–1, 85, 88–9, 95–7,
    103, 105, 110, 121, 138,
    152–3, 172, 173, 177
Doughty, P. L. 93
Downing, T. E. 92

Draft Declaration on the
    Rights of Indigenous
    Peoples 122
duties 16, 20, 26, 36, 41,
    58–9, 73, 75, 103–4, 112
Dworkin, R. 61, 69, 72

early warning 175
East Asia 87–9, 163
Economic and Social Council
    44, 143
economic and social rights 30,
    39–41, 46, 47, 51, 52, 71,
    72, 95, 98, 105, 139, 141,
    147, 148–51, 153, 156–8,
    161, 164–6, 168, 171,
    176, 177
economic development 80–1,
    138–9, 140, 149–50, 153,
    156, 158, 162, 163, 170
Eide, A. 164
El Salvador 164
equality 23, 25–6, 37, 89,
    107–8, 111, 112, 115–16,
    119, 129
explanation 6, 78

family 38, 104, 129
fascism 4, 39, 68–9, 169
Fein, H. 140
feminism 63, 127–30
feminization of poverty 154
foreign direct investment 156,
    157–8
foreign policy 95–7, 133–4,
    137, 157, 177
Forsythe, D. 56–7, 75, 132–3,
    144–5
foundations, theoretical *see*
    source of human rights
Foweraker, J. and Landman, T.
    82–3, 139–40, 142
Franciscans 18
freedom of expression 38–9

freedom of religion 4, 21, 38
free markets 149, 151, 153,
    163, 166, 176
French Revolution 24–5, 27,
    37, 54, 169
frustration-aggression theory
    91

Gandhi, M. 58
Gewirth, A. 57, 70, 73, 75
global compact 159
globalization 51, 83–4, 88,
    110, 153–61, 163, 166,
    171, 173, 178
good governance 151, 162
Goodin, R. 149
Grotius, H. 18
Gurr, T. R. 81–2, 139

Held, D. 154
Helsinki Final Act 47, 94–5,
    170
Henderson, C. W. 140
High Commissioner for
    Human Rights 51, 53
history, value of 14, 172
Hobbes, T. 19
Howard, R. 85–7, 88
human development index 164
human nature 59, 64–6, 68
Human Rights Commission
    34–5, 43, 44, 49, 76, 122,
    152
Human Rights Committee 45,
    123
human rights education 146,
    178
human rights movement
    159–60, 171, 176
Human Rights Watch 144
human rights violations 1–2

idealism 131, 170, 172
Idéologues 29

imperialism 104, 107–11, 154
indigenous peoples 120, 121–3
individualism 21–2, 25, 29, 36, 56, 73, 86, 89, 103, 107, 114, 115–18, 123, 124–5, 171
indivisibility 40–1, 51, 54, 105, 142, 148, 172
inequality 22, 25–6, 85, 89, 120, 151, 163, 171
International Bill of Rights 45
International Covenant on Civil and Political Rights 40, 45, 104, 114–15
International Covenant on Economic, Social and Cultural Rights 45, 52, 164
International Criminal Tribunal for the Former Yugoslavia 50, 132
international financial institutions 157, 160–4, 172, 173, 174, 177
International Labour Organization 32, 39, 52, 122, 127, 142, 164
international law 8
International Monetary Fund 149, 153, 155, 160–2
intervention 94, 97, 106, 119–20, 133–4, 174–6
Iraq 175
Islam 111–13

justice 73–4, 103, 119, 126, 152
justiciability 165
justification 6, 10–11, 41–2, 55–60, 68, 70

Kant, I. 24
Kosovo 175, 176

Kuwait 175
Kymlicka, W. 116–18, 123

League of Nations 30–1, 32, 40, 114
legal analysis 4, 6, 12, 58, 77–9, 83, 87, 132, 171, 175, 177
legal positivism 10, 42
legal rights 5, 10, 28, 37, 60, 62
Levellers 19
liberal democracy 119–20
liberalism 35–8, 42, 64–5, 67, 73, 87, 88–9, 103–4, 108, 115–19, 124–5, 129
limits of human rights 11, 61–3, 69–70, 74, 75, 118
lip service 135
Locke, J. 7, 10, 21–2, 35, 36, 37, 73, 103, 107, 108, 115, 168, 177

Macdonald, M. 59
Macedonia 174
McGrew, A. G. 159–60
MacIntyre, A. 5–6, 15
Macpherson, C. B. 22
Magna Carta 17, 168
majority rule 117
Malaysia 113
Margalit, A. and Raz, J. 125
Maritain, J. 58, 75
Marx, K. 29, 56, 57, 172
M'Baye, K. 151
Messer, E. 93
Meyer, W. 157–8
Miller, D. 126
Miller, F. 167
Milner, W. T. 141–2
Milosevic, Slobodan 174
minimum standards 11, 118
minimum threshold approach 164

minorities 32–3, 40, 114–21, 124
Mitchell, N. J. and McCormick, J. M. 140, 157
mobilization of shame 145
modernization 64, 86, 88, 105, 137
Moon, B. 158
multiculturalism 116
multinational corporations 51, 63, 98, 132, 151, 154–60, 162, 171–2, 173, 174
murder in the middle 140

nationalism 125–6
nation-states 126–7, 178
NATO 50, 174
natural law 18–22, 27, 55–6, 59–60, 73, 74, 76, 103–4, 167
Nazism 33, 35, 37, 38, 54, 59, 95, 104, 114, 155, 172, 175
needs 65, 158
neo-liberalism 153, 156–7, 163–4, 177
New International Economic Order 47, 148, 153
non-governmental organizations (NGOs) 43, 45–7, 52, 53, 82, 98, 130, 132–3, 135, 137, 142–7, 153–5, 158–9, 161–3, 165–6, 171, 173, 175, 178
Nussbaum, M. 65–8, 75, 177

obedience to authority 91
objective right 16, 18, 103
obligations, human-rights 63
Organization for Security and Co-operation in Europe (OSCE) 47
Othman, N. 111–12

Paine, T. 25
patriarchalism 87–9
Poe, S. C. and Tate, C. N. 140
political economy 173, 177
positivism 59, 76, 78, 81, 83, 92, 98, 99–100
power 74, 85, 87, 100, 107, 117, 119, 155, 167, 171, 177, 178
principle of limited sacrifice 134, 171, 175
property 17–19, 22, 38, 71, 76, 82, 125, 168
Protestantism 20, 169
public good 21–2, 26, 68–9, 167

racism 104, 159, 170
realism 7, 78, 84, 94, 96, 131–2, 134, 136–7, 158, 171
reason 20–1, 24, 25–6, 55–6, 59, 169
regime, human rights 53–4, 95–6, 131–2, 138, 147, 153–5, 159
Renaissance 18
rescue, psychology of 91–2
Resolution 1235 44–5
Resolution 1503 44–5
rights 5, 60–1
rights inflation 5
Rights of Man 25, 55
right to development 47, 151–3
right to self-determination 122–7, 154
Risse, T. 98, 134–8, 173, 178
Roman law 16
Rorty, R. 56, 75
Rousseau, J.-J. 115
Rwanda 50, 52, 170, 173, 175, 176

Saint-Simon 29
scapegoat theory 91
Schirmer, J. 93
secession 126–7
secularization 19, 23–4, 26,
    55, 83, 111, 169
Security Council 133, 174
self-emancipation 112–13,
    119–20
self-entrapment 136
self-preservation 17, 19
Sen, A. 150, 177
Shehadi, K. S. 126
Shue, H. 70, 71
slavery 32, 37, 43, 142
Smith, J. 158
social constructivism 68, 70,
    84, 153, 172
social democracy 67
social movements 82–3, 85,
    86, 98, 138, 139–40, 147,
    160
Somalia 49
source of human rights 10–11,
    35–6, 41–2, 56, 58–9, 75,
    110
South Korea 80–1, 138–9, 149
sovereignty 9, 34, 43, 51, 53,
    109, 132, 134, 154–6,
    161–2, 173–4
Stammers, N. 85
states 4, 26, 53–4, 63–4, 82,
    85–6, 94–7, 105, 128,
    131, 133, 137, 138–9,
    152, 153–6, 161, 163,
    165, 171, 173, 178
state violence 81–2
statistics 2, 80, 140–2, 157
Steiner, H. 71
Stoics 17, 167
Stoll, D. 94
structural adjustment
    programmes 149, 161
structural analysis 171–2

Sub-Commission on Prevention
    of Discrimination and
    Protection of Minorities
    114
subjective rights 16, 18
subsistence 22, 39, 95, 168
Survival International 92
sympathy 2, 4, 56, 75, 90,
    99

Taiwan 149
territorial integrity 124, 126,
    154, 161
thematic procedures 46
third-generation rights 47–8,
    148, 168
Thomas, C. 163
Tierney, B. 17, 168
toleration 119
torture 37, 141
trade-offs 80, 138–9, 151
trumps, rights as 61, 69
trust 19, 21
Tully, J. 118–19
Turner, B. S. 83
tyranny 16, 21

United Nations 9, 33, 43,
    50–2, 54, 55–6, 59, 133,
    155, 159, 161, 164, 169,
    171, 177, 178
UN Charter 33–4, 127, 142–
    3
UN Development Programme
    153
UNESCO 58, 77–8
UN High Commissioner for
    Refugees (UNHCR) 50
United States Constitution 23
Universal Declaration of
    Human Rights 3, 10–11,
    32, 34–43, 45, 53–4,
    57, 61, 76–7, 84, 88,
    101, 104–5, 114–15, 118,

127, 128, 129, 142, 169, 178

universalism 20, 25, 27, 44, 48, 51, 65, 93, 101–2, 104, 105–9, 112, 120, 167, 172, 173

USA 105, 132, 140, 157

USSR 81, 140

Utilitarianism 28, 30, 33, 68–9

Vienna conference 48, 51, 53, 71, 101–2, 105, 127, 128, 143, 148, 170, 173

Virginia Declaration of Rights 23

Villey, M. 16

Vincent, R. J. 94–5

Waldron, J. 72

Waters, M. 84

welfare 26, 71, 156

Western, human rights as 36, 37, 103, 108, 110–11, 132, 146–7, 160, 172

Wilson, R. A. 93

Wollstonecraft, M. 23

Woodiwiss, A. 87–9

women's rights 23, 63–4, 89, 127–30, 154, 176

Working Group on Indigenous Peoples 122

World Bank 149, 153, 155, 156, 160–3

World Conference on Women 1995 130, 143

World Health Organization 164

World Trade Organization 149, 151, 156, 159, 160

Yugoslavia 49–50, 81, 82, 97, 133, 174, 177

Zanger, S. 141